THE DESTINY
OF THE NATIONS

BOOKS BY ALICE A. BAILEY

THE DESTINY
OF
THE NATIONS

By
Alice A. Bailey

LUCIS PUBLISHING COMPANY
113 University Place, 11th Floor
P.O. Box 722, Cooper Station
New York, N.Y. 10276

LUCIS PRESS LTD.
Suite 54
3 Whitehall Court
London SW1A 2EF
England

First Printing, 1949
Sixth Printing, 1978
Eighth Printing, 1990 (4th Paperback Edition)

ISBN NO. 0-85330-102-6
Library of Congress Catalog Card Number: 89-195778

The publication of this book is financed by the Tibetan Book Fund which is established for the perpetuation of the teachings of the Tibetan and Alice A. Bailey.

This Fund is controlled by the Lucis Trust, a tax-exempt, religious, educational corporation.

The Lucis Publishing Company is a non-profit organisation owned by the Lucis Trust. No royalties are paid on this book.

This title is also available in a
clothbound edition.

It has been translated into Danish, Dutch, French, German, Greek, Italian, Portuguese and Spanish. Translation into other languages is proceeding.

MANUFACTURED IN THE UNITED STATES OF AMERICA
By FORT ORANGE PRESS, INC., Albany, N.Y.

EXTRACT FROM A STATEMENT BY THE TIBETAN

Suffice it to say, that I am a Tibetan disciple of a certain degree, and this tells you but little, for all are disciples from the humblest aspirant up to, and beyond, the Christ Himself. I live in a physical body like other men, on the borders of Tibet, and at times (from the exoteric standpoint) preside over a large group of Tibetan lamas, when my other duties permit. It is this fact that has caused it to be reported that I am an abbot of this particular lamasery. Those associated with me in the work of the Hierarchy (and all true disciples are associated in this work) know me by still another name and office. A.A.B. knows who I am and recognises me by two of my names.

I am a brother of yours, who has travelled a little longer upon the Path than has the average student, and has therefore incurred greater responsibilities. I am one who has wrestled and fought his way into a greater measure of light than has the aspirant who will read this article, and I must therefore act as a transmitter of the light, no matter what the cost. I am not an old man, as age counts among the teachers, yet I am not young or inexperienced. My work is to teach and spread the knowledge of the Ageless Wisdom wherever I can find a response, and I have been doing this for many years. I seek also to help the Master M. and the Master K.H. whenever opportunity offers, for I have been long connected with Them and with Their work. In all the above, I have told you much; yet at the same time I have told you nothing which would lead you to offer me that blind obedience and the foolish devotion which the emotional aspirant offers to the Guru and Master Whom he is as yet unable to contact. Nor will he make that desired contact until he has transmuted emotional devotion into unselfish service to humanity,—not to the Master.

The books that I have written are sent out with no claim for their acceptance. They may, or may not, be correct, true and useful. It is for you to ascertain their truth by right practice and by the exercise of the intuition. Neither I nor A.A.B. is the least interested in having them acclaimed as inspired writings, or in having anyone speak of them (with bated breath) as being the work of one of the Masters. If they present truth in such a way that it follows sequentially upon that already offered in the world teachings, if the information given raises the aspiration and the will-to-serve from the plane of the emotions to that of the mind (the plane whereon the Masters *can* be found) then they will have served their purpose. If the teaching conveyed calls forth a response from the illumined mind of the worker in the world, and brings a flashing forth of his intuition, then let that teaching be accepted. But not otherwise. If the statements meet with eventual corroboration, or are deemed true under the test of the Law of Correspondences, then that is well and good. But should this not be so, let not the student accept what is said.

AUGUST 1934

THE GREAT INVOCATION

From the point of Light within the Mind of God
    Let light stream forth into the minds of men.
      Let Light descend on Earth.

From the point of Love within the Heart of God
    Let love stream forth into the hearts of men.
      May Christ return to Earth.

From the centre where the Will of God is known
    Let purpose guide the little wills of men —
      The purpose which the Masters know and serve.

From the centre which we call the race of men
    Let the Plan of Love and Light work out
      And may it seal the door where evil dwells.

Let Light and Love and Power restore the Plan on Earth.

"The above Invocation or Prayer does not belong to any person or group but to all Humanity. The beauty and the strength of this Invocation lies in its simplicity, and in its expression of certain central truths which all men, innately and normally, accept—the truth of the existence of a basic Intelligence to Whom we vaguely give the name of God; the truth that behind all outer seeming, the motivating power of the universe is Love; the truth that a great Individuality came to earth, called by Christians, the Christ, and embodied that love so that we could understand; the truth that both love and intelligence are effects of what is called the Will of God; and finally the self-evident truth that only through *humanity* itself can the Divine Plan work out."

ALICE A. BAILEY

TABLE OF CONTENTS

THE DESTINY OF THE NATIONS

Introduction

It is of major interest for us to know something about the energies and forces which are producing the present international situation and presenting the complex problems with which the United Nations are confronted. In the last analysis, all history is the record of the effects of these energies or radiations (rays, in other words) as they play upon humanity in its many varying stages of evolutionary development. These stages extend all the way from those of primeval humanity to our modern civilisation; all that has happened is the result of these energies, pouring cyclically through nature and through that part of nature which we call the human kingdom.

To understand what is today taking place we must recognise that these energies are seven in number. They are called by many names in many different lands, but for our purposes the following seven names will be used:

1. The energy of Will, Purpose or Power, called in Christian lands the energy of the Will of God.
2. The energy of Love-Wisdom, called frequently the Love of God.
3. The energy of Active Intelligence, called the Mind of God.
4. The energy of Harmony through Conflict, affecting greatly the human family.
5. The energy of Concrete Knowledge or Science, so potent at this time.
6. The energy of Devotion or Idealism, producing the current ideologies.

7. The energy of Ceremonial Order, producing the new forms of civilisation.

These energies are ceaselessly playing on humanity, producing changes, expressing themselves through successive civilisations and cultures, and fashioning the many races and nations.

This in no way infringes upon man's freewill; these forces have both their higher and their lower aspects and men respond to them according to their mental and spiritual development, and so do nations and races as a whole. Humanity has reached a point today where there is a most sensitive response to that which is higher and better.

This teaching anent the seven rays remains a profitless speculation unless it is susceptible of investigation, of eventual proof and of general as well as particular usefulness. Too much is written at this time which will have to be relegated to the discard as useless, as not warranting acceptance as a possible hypothesis and as not demonstrating a truth which can be proved. I am, therefore, seeking here to do two things:

1. Indicate, as you have seen, a new and powerfully efficient esoteric psychology, and also
2. Show the lines of development which are inevitable, for the reason that certain major potencies are coming into play at this time. Certain forces are becoming increasingly active whilst others are steadily becoming quiescent. It is these active forces which we will now consider.

I would like to pause here and point out that these forces come into play either cyclically or through demand. This is an interesting point for students to remember. The work done through the Great Invocation is not then necessarily invalid. It might perhaps clarify the subject if I pointed out that there are five energies (and there are usually five dominant ray energies active at any time) coming into play:

1. Those energies which are passing out of manifestation, as the sixth Ray of Devotion is at this time passing out.
2. Those energies which are coming into manifestation or incarnation, as the seventh Ray of Ceremonial Order is at this time emerging into expression.
3. Those energies which are—at any given time—express∙ing the ray type of the bulk of the manifesting humanity. Today these ray types are predominantly the second and the third. Relatively large numbers of first ray egos are also to be found acting as focal points for certain first ray forces.
4. Those energies which are today being invoked as the result of human need and human demand for succor. This demand curiously enough remains largely in the realm of the first ray influence for the desperate need of humanity is evoking the will aspect and that ray embodies the divine will-to-good and remains immutable and is—for the first time in the history of humanity—being invoked on a large scale. This statement is definitely encouraging, if you study its implications.

You have, therefore, in the present field of divine expression the following energies manifesting:

1. The energy of idealism, of devotion or of devoted attention, embodied in the sixth ray.
2. The energy whose major function it is to produce order, rhythm and established, sequential activity—the seventh Ray of Ceremonial Ritual.
3. The energy of the second ray, which is always basically

present in our solar system, that of love-wisdom, to which many of the egos now in incarnation belong and will increasingly belong. The next one hundred and fifty years will see them coming into incarnation. The reason is that it is to this type of human being that the work of reconstruction, and of re-building is naturally committed.

4. The energy of intelligence, actively displayed in creative activity. The creative ability of the future will emerge on a relatively large scale in the realm of creative living and not so much in the realm of creative art. This creative living will express itself through a new world of beauty and of recognised divine expression; through the outer form, the "light of livingness" (as it is esoterically called) will show. The symbol and that for which it stands will be known and seen. This is the energy of the third Ray of Active Intelligence, working towards the manifestation of beauty.

5. The energy of the will aspect of divinity. This has been but little expressed and understood by humanity up to the present, but the time has now come when it must be better comprehended. The demand from our innumerable planetary forces has not hitherto been adequate to invoke it and for its invocation the great Lord of the World has patiently waited. The call has now gone forth. Its first faint notes were heard two hundred years ago and the sound and demand has increased in volume and potency until today this great energy is making its presence unmistakably felt.

I am anxious to have you realise the potency and the effect of these five energies as they play upon our planet, evoke response—good and bad—and produce the turmoil and chaos, the warring forces and the beneficent influences. They, therefore, account in their totality for all that we see happening around us at this time. In the books which are being written today in an effort to solve the problems of the why and the wherefore of present world conditions, the writers are necessarily dealing only with effects. Few there are that can penetrate into the distant world of causes or look back into that ancient past and see past and present in their true perspective. I, however, seek to deal with causes— predisposing, effective, determining, and productive of those events which cause the present state of affairs. I deal with energies; they are concerned with resultant forces. I would remind you here that these effects which are producing so much fear, foreboding and concern are but temporary and will give place to that ordered, rhythmic imposition of the needed idealism which will be applied eventually by love, motivated by wisdom in cooperation with intelligence. All will be actuated by a dynamic (not a passive) will-to-good.

We will divide what I have to say under two points:

1. The situation and its ray causes in the immediate present.
2. The situation in the future when the Aquarian Age is really established and the Piscean influences are no longer dominant.

Before we take up these points, however, I have a few introductory comments to make. These it is essential that you should study and comprehend for upon their right acceptance and understanding will depend the benefit you will gain from my teaching upon these points.

It is a truism to remark that the history of the world is based on the emergence of ideas, their acceptance, their transformation into ideals, and their eventual superseding by the next imposition of ideas. It is in this realm of *ideas* that humanity is not a free agent. This is an important point to note. Once an idea becomes an ideal, humanity can freely reject or accept it, but ideas come from a higher source and are *imposed* upon the racial mind, whether men want them or not. Upon the use made of these ideas (which are in the nature of divine emanations, embodying the divine plan for planetary progress) will depend the rapidity of humanity's progress or its retardation for lack of understanding.

Humanity is today more sensitive to ideas than ever before, and hence the many warring ideologies and hence the fact that—in defence of their plans—even the most recalcitrant of the nations has to discover some idealistic excuse to put before the other nations when occupied with any infringement of recognised law. This is a fact of great significance to the Hierarchy for it indicates a point reached. The major ideas in the world today fall into five categories which it would be well for you to bear in mind:

1. The ancient and inherited ideas which have controlled the racial life for centuries—aggression for the sake of possession and the authority of a man or a group or a church which represents the State. For purposes of policy such powers may work behind the scenes but their tenets and motives are easily recognisable—selfish ambition and a violently imposed authority.

2. Those ideas which are relatively new such as Nazism, Fascism, and Communism, though they are not really as new as people are apt to think. They are alike on one important point, i.e. The State or community of human beings counts as of importance whilst the individual does not; he can be sacrificed at any time for the good of the State or for the so-called general good.

3. The idea, neither old nor particularly new, of democracy in which (supposedly but as yet never factually) the people govern and the government represents the will of the people.

4. The idea of a world state, divided into various great sections. This is the dream of the inclusively-minded few, for which many regard humanity as yet unready. Towards this the entire world is headed in spite of its many ideologies, each fighting with each other for supremacy and oblivious of the important fact that all these ideologies may be temporarily adapted to the groups or nations who adopt them. They are none of them suitable for general use (and I say this equally of democracy as of any other ideology); they suit well in all probability the nations who accept them and mould their national life on their premises; they are only transitory substitutes in this transition period between the Piscean and the Aquarian ages and cannot permanently last. Nothing as yet is permanent. When permanency is reached, evolution will cease and God's plan will be consummated. And then? The greatest revelation of all will come at the close of this world period when the human mind, intuition and soul consciousness is such that understanding will be possible.

5. The idea of a spiritual Hierarchy which will govern the people throughout the world and will embody in itself the best elements of the monarchial, the democratic, the totalitarian and the communistic regimes. *Most of these groups of ideologies have latent in them much beauty, strength and wisdom, and also a profound and valuable contribution to make to the whole*. Each will eventually see its contribution embodied under the control of the Hierarchy of the Lords of Compassion and

the Masters of the Wisdom. The restoration of the
ancient Atlantean control by the spiritual forces is still
in the future but the Aquarian Age will see the restitu-
tion of this inner and spiritual guidance on a higher turn
of the spiral.

All this must inevitably be brought about by the work of
those who function on one or other of the five controlling
rays to which I have referred above. Nothing can stop or
truly impede their united effect. This is a point I would have
you remember. Modern man is apt to condemn the ideology
which is not familiar to him and for which he has no use.
He repudiates those ideas which do not lie at the back of
his national and personal life or tradition and which would
not suit him as an individual nor meet the need of the nation
to which he belongs.

The recognition of these facts would lead to two results
if correctly applied: first, the individual who accepts and is
devoted to a particular ideology would cease fighting other
ideologies for he would remember that the accident of birth
and of background is largely responsible for making him—
as an individual—what he is and determining his beliefs.
And, secondly, it would bring to an end the attempt to
impose a personally or nationally accepted ideology (political or religious) on other nations and persons. These are
basic steps towards eventual peace and understanding and
hence I emphasise them today.

It will be of value next if I connect up the three major
planetary centres of energy with the five rays which are today working towards the consummation of the Plan for
the race at this time. Three of these streams of energy are
working powerfully in the world at this time and two
others are struggling for expression. Of these latter, one is

struggling towards domination and the other is struggling to hold on to that which it has so long controlled. This refers to the incoming seventh ray and the outgoing sixth ray. They constitute, in their duality, the reactionary and the progressive forces which are seeking to govern human thought, to determine natural and human evolution and to produce widely divergent civilisations and culture—one of which would be the perpetuation and crystallisation of that which now exists and the other would be so entirely new, as an outgrowth of the present world upheaval, that it is difficult for the average student to conceive of its nature.

These five energies together will determine the trend of world affairs. The problem before the Hierarchy at this time is so to direct and control these powerful activities that the Plan can be rightly materialised and the close of this century and the beginning of the next see the purposes of God for the planet and for humanity assume right direction and proportion. In this way, the new culture for the relatively few and the new civilisation for the many during the coming age will start in such a manner that the peoples of the earth can go forward into an era of peace and true development—spiritual and material. I would like to remind you that the fact that you see the world picture as one of outstanding chaos, of striving ideologies and warring forces, of the persecution of minorities, of hatreds which are working out into a furious preparation for war, and of world anxiety and terror does not really mean that you are seeing the picture as it is in reality. You are seeing what is superficial, temporal, ephemeral and entirely concerned with the form aspect. The Hierarchy is primarily occupied, as you know well, with the consciousness aspect and with the unfoldment of awareness, using form as a means only for the accomplishment of its designs. A closer study of the forces which are producing the outer turmoil may serve to clarify your vision and restore confidence in God's plan and its divine love and loveliness. Let us, therefore, consider these forces and their originating centres, and thus acquire perhaps a new vision and a more constructive point of view.

1. The Influence of the Rays Today.

First: The most obvious and powerful force in the world today is that of the *first Ray of Will and Power*. It works out in two ways:

1. As the will of God in world affairs, which is ever the will-to-good. Steadily—if you study human history intelligently—you will see that there has been a regular and rhythmic progression toward unity and synthesis in all departments of human affairs. This unity in multiplicity is the Eternal Plan—a unity in consciousness, a multiplicity in form.

2. As the destructive element in world affairs. This refers to man's use of this force of will which is seldom as yet the will-to-good in active expression, but something which leads to self-assertion (of the individual or the nation) and to war with its accompaniments—separation, selfish diplomacy, hate and armaments, disease and death.

This is the force which pours into the world from the major world centre, *Shamballa*. Little is known of Shamballa. More will be known as you study this text and note how world affairs are taking shape before your eyes in accordance with my prevision (as presented to your limited vision) and the obvious possibilities. These are necessarily the equally obvious effects of the predisposing causes.

Only twice before in the history of mankind has this Shamballa energy made its appearance and caused its presence to be felt through the tremendous changes which were brought about:

1. When the first great human crisis occurred at the time of the individualisation of man in ancient Lemuria.

2. At the time of the great struggle in Atlantean days between the "Lords of Light and the Lords of Material Expression."

This little known divine energy now streams out from the Holy Centre. It embodies in itself the energy which lies behind the world crisis of the moment. It is the *Will* of God to produce certain radical and momentous changes in the consciousness of the race which will completely alter man's attitude to life and his grasp of the spiritual, esoteric and subjective essentials of living. It is this force which will bring about (in conjunction with second ray force) that tremendous crisis—imminent in the human consciousness—which we call the second crisis, *the initiation* of the race into the Mystery of the Ages, into that which has been hid from the beginning.

The first crisis, as you have been taught, was the crisis of individualisation wherein man became a living soul. The second crisis is the immediate one of racial initiation, made possible (if you will but believe it) by the many individual initiations which have lately been undergone by those members of the human family who had vision and a willingness to pay the price.

This particular and somewhat unusual ray energy is expressing itself in two ways. Perhaps it would be more correct to say in two ways that are recognisable by man, because it should be remembered that these ray forces express themselves as potently in other kingdoms in nature as they do in the human. For instance, one phase of the destructive aspect of first ray force has been the organised and scientific destruction of forms in the animal kingdom. This is the destroying force, as manipulated by man. Another phase of the same force (which can be noted in relation to the unfoldment of consciousness in subtle and powerful ways) can be seen in the effect which human beings have upon the domestic animals, hastening their evolution, and stimulating them into forms of advanced instinctual activity. I mention these two phases as illustration of the effect of first ray energy in the animal kingdom, as expressed through human activity.

The ways in which humanity itself is affected by this ray energy, as it expresses itself in a twofold manner, producing a twofold result, are as follows:

1. There is, at this time, an emergence of certain powerful and dominating first ray personalities into the theatre of world activity. These people are in direct contact with this Shamballa force and are sensitive to the impact of the will energy of Deity. According to their type of personality and their point in evolution will be their reaction to this force and their consequent usefulness to the Lord of the World as He works out His plans of world unfoldment. The energy of the will of God works through them, though stepped down and often misused and misapplied, by their differing and limited personalities, and interpreted unsatisfactorily by their undeveloped consciousnesses. These people are found in every

field of human affairs. They are the dominant persons, and the dictators in every aspect of human living—political, social, religious and educational. Who shall say (until at least a century has gone by) whether their influence and their efforts have been good or bad. Where they flagrantly infringe the Law of Love, their influence may be powerful, but it is passing and undesirable, at least where that phase of their activities is concerned. Where they meet human emergency and need, and work along lines of basic restoration and the preservation of "units of synthesis," their influence is good and constructive.

I would here point out that real group love never demonstrates as hatred of the individual. It may work out as the arresting of the individual's activities or enterprises where that is deemed desirable in the interests of the whole and if what he is doing is estimated as harmful to the good of the group. But the arresting will not be destructive. It will be educational and developing in its results.

The true first ray personality who works in response to this Shamballa influence will have the ultimate good of the group deeply enshrined in his consciousness and heart; he will think in terms of the whole and not in terms of the part. That is the thing which he will endeavour to impress upon the racial consciousness. This may lead at times to ruthlessness and cruelty if the personality of the individual is not yet controlled by soul impulse. Such cases can frequently be seen. An instance of this can be noted in the history of the Jews as found in the Old Testament. When the first ray was in control and passing through one of its rare cycles of activity we read that they butchered and slaughtered all their enemies—men, women and children, putting them to the sword. The sword is ever the symbol of the first ray force just as the pen is of the second ray influence.

I wish to remind you that I use the word "energy" in reference to the spiritual expression of any ray and the word "force" to denote the use which men make of spiritual energy as they seek to employ it and usually, as yet, misapply it. I would point out that Ataturk, the Turkish dictator, within certain personality limitations of relatively negligible moment, made good use of first ray energy, and only the testimony of future historical records will indicate fully how wisely, sanely and disinterestedly he used this type of force for the attainment of first ray objectives. It might be apposite here to point out that such first ray exponents of force are often misunderstood and hated. They may and often do misuse the energy available but they also use it constructively within the desired limits of the immediate plan. I would also like to state that the lot of a first ray disciple is hard and difficult. There are disciples of Shamballa just as there are disciples of the Hierarchy and this is a fact hitherto not recognised and never as yet referred to in the current writings on occult subjects. It is wise and valuable to remember this. They are powerful, these disciples of Shamballa, headstrong and often cruel; they impose their will and dictate their desires; they make mistakes but they are nevertheless true disciples of Shamballa and are working out the Will of God as much as the disciples and Masters of the Hierarchy are working out the Love of God.

This is a hard saying for some of you but your failure to recognise this truth and to respond to it does not affect the issue. It simply makes your individual lot and difficulties harder.

I would also remind you that the use of first ray energy inevitably means destruction in the early stages but fusion and blending in the later and final results. If you study the nations of the world today from this angle, you will see this Shamballa energy of will working out potently through the agency of certain great outstanding personalities. The Lord of Shamballa in this time of urgency, from love of the life aspect and from understanding of the Plan as well as from love of humanity, is sending forth this dynamic energy. It is form destroying and brings death to those material forms and organised bodies which hinder the free expression of the life of God, for they negate the new culture and render inactive the seeds of the coming civilisation.

From this display of energy, unthinking humanity draws back in fear and likes it not. When full of personality hate and self-will, human beings seek often to turn this energy to their own selfish ends. If human beings (even the best of them) were not so undeveloped and so superficial in their judgments and their vision, they would be able to penetrate behind what is going on in the key countries in the world and see the gradual emergence of new and better conditions, and the passing away of the loved, but slowly decaying forms. The energy of Shamballa is, however, so new and so strange that it is hard for human beings to know it for what it is—the demonstration of the Will of God in new and potent livingness.

2. The second way in which this dominant will impulse makes itself felt is through the voice of the masses of the people throughout the world. This will express itself through *sound*, as consciousness or love does through *light*. The sound of the nations has been heard as a mass sound for the first time. That voice today is un-

mistakably expressive of the values which embody human betterment; it demands peace and understanding between men and it refuses—and will steadily refuse—to permit certain drastic things to happen. This "voice of the people," which is in reality the voice of public opinion is, for the first time and with no recognition of the fact, being determined by the Will of God.

Second: The next great energy which is making its potent contribution to the present world situation is that of the *second Ray of Love Wisdom, Christ's ray*. This energy is poured into the world through the second great planetary centre which we call The Hierarchy. The energy which is concentrated in this centre and which is manipulated by the initiates and the Masters is making one of its cyclic impacts upon the Earth and—as I explained in Volume II of *A Treatise on the Seven Rays*—is also making one of its major cyclic Approaches to humanity.

The energy flowing through the Hierarchy at this time —the energy of love—is seeking to blend with that which is flowing out of Shamballa and is needed in order to make the desired application of it. The problem of the Hierarchy at this time is to produce a wise and adequate fusion of the Shamballa and the hierarchial energies and thus temper destruction and bring to the fore the spirit of construction, setting in motion the building and re-habilitating forces of the second ray energy. The Shamballa energy prepares the way for the energy of the Hierarchy. Thus it has been from the beginning of time, but the cycles of the Hierarchy, though relatively frequent, have not coincided with those of Shamballa, which are rare and infrequent. As time progresses, the impact of the Shamballa force will be more frequent because men will develop the power to stand and withstand it. Hitherto it has been too dangerous an energy to apply to mankind, for the results have worked out destructively, except in the first great Lemurian crisis. Its work has, therefore, been confined almost entirely to the Hierarchy Whose Members are equipped to handle it and to assimilate it correctly and also to use it for the benefit of humanity. Now the experiment is being attempted of permitting man to receive it and, its impact, free from the mediation of the Hierarchy. It may prove a premature and abortive effort but the issues are not yet determined and the Lord of Shamballa, with His assistants and with the aid of the watching Members of the Hierarchy, are not discouraged over the initial results. Humanity is responding unexpectedly well. There has been much success along this line but the results do not appear with clarity to intelligent human beings because they refuse to see anything except the destructive aspect and the disappearance of the forms to which they have hitherto anchored their emotions, their desire, and their mental perceptions. They fail, as yet, to see the irrefutable evidence of constructive activity and of true creative work. The temple of humanity in the New Age is rising rapidly but its outlines cannot be seen because men are occupied entirely with their individual or national selfish point of view and with their personal or national instincts and impulses. I would here like to call your attention to the fact that the instinctual life of nations is something which remains to be studied scientifically and is a phase which leads inevitably to the individualistic life of nations— a matter of more immediate interest.

The new forms are, however, being built and the Shamballa potencies, plus hierarchical guidance, are working towards ends which are definitely planned and which are working out favourably. The potency of love-wisdom, transmitted by the Hierarchy, is playing upon modern humanity in a more intimate and close manner than ever before. The Directors of the Hierarchy are seeking to evoke an intelligent response from men and an indication that they are *conscious* of what is happening. Most of the response to the Shamballa activity is characterised by fear and terror, by sensitivity and distressingly developed reactions to the forces of hate and separation. Only a few, here and there, really grasp the vision of the future and realise what is going on, seeing truly the beauty of the emerging plan. It is with these few that the Members of the Hierarchy can work because they (even when lacking understanding) bear no ill-will or hatred to others. Love is a great unifier and interpreter.

This energy of love is primarily concentrated (for purposes of hierarchical activity) in the New Group of World Servers. This group has been chosen by the Hierarchy as its main channel of expression. This group, composed as it is of all world disciples and all working initiates, finds its representatives in every group of idealists and servers and in every body of people who express human thought, particularly in the realm of human betterment and uplift. Through them, the potency of love-wisdom can express itself. These people are frequently misunderstood, for the love which they express differs widely from the sentimental, affectionate personal interest of the average worker. They are occupied mainly with the interests and the good of the whole group with which they may be associated; they are not primarily concerned with the petty interests of the individual—occupied with his little problems and concerns. This brings such a server under the criticism of the individual and with this criticism they must learn to live and to it they must pay no attention. True group love is of more importance than personal relationships, though those are met as need (note, I say, *need*) arises. Disciples learn to grasp the need of group love and to amend their ways in conformity with group good, but it is not easy for the self-interested individual to grasp the difference. Through the medium of those disciples who have learned the distinction between the petty concerns of the individual plus his interest in himself and the necessities and urgencies of group work and love, the Hierarchy can work and so bring about the needed world changes, which are primarily *changes in consciousness*. I have dealt somewhat in detail with these matters; the gist of them has, however, been embodied in the pamphlets sent out in the past few years.

Third: the major energy upon which we shall touch here is that of *intelligent activity*—the potency of the third ray. This finds its expression through the third major centre on the planet; this centre, we call Humanity. The evocation of a loving intelligent response to the Shamballa impulse, stepped down by the Hierarchy, is that to which this world centre should respond. This is rapidly and, as I have told you, satisfactorily, happening. A definite world effect is being produced and the New Group of World Servers has given much aid in this. They have interpreted, explained and assisted the processes of evoking the latent love in human beings which, in its initial and unformed stages, exists in the form of an inchoate goodwill.

I call this to your attention as the underlying, motivating idea behind all the work which you are called upon to do. I suggest, therefore, that you endeavour to see the three major ideologies with which you have perforce to deal in terms of the three efforts which are emanating from the three major planetary centres at this time: Shamballa, the Hierarchy and Humanity. You will thus gain a more synthetic viewpoint, and a deeper understanding of the slowly emerging world picture.

Is it not possible that the ideologies which we have been discussing are the response—distorted and yet a definite and determined, sensitive reaction—to the energies playing upon humanity from the two higher major centres? I would like to suggest that the ideology which is embodied in the vision of the totalitarian states is an erroneous but clear-cut response to the Shamballa influence of *will*; that the ideology behind the democratic ideal constitutes a similar response to the universality which the *love* of the Hierarchy prompts it to express, and that communism is of human origin, embodying that ideology which humanity has formulated in its own right. Thus the three aspects of God's nature are beginning to take form as three major ideas and what we see upon the planet at this time are the distorted human reactions to spiritual impulses, emanating from three different centres, but all equally divine in their essential natures, and in their essences. Ponder on this.

I have brought this to your attention and discussed these basic modern schools of thought because the potency of their idealism is affecting every person, capable of thought, upon the planet. Not one of you is immune from their effects; not one of you but is inclined to range yourself upon one side or another, fighting furiously and under the cloak of so-called "adherence to principle" for what appeals to you. Most of you are, nevertheless, far more affected by the methods employed to materialise the ideas and by the quality of their exponents than you are by the ideas themselves. These you could hardly define if asked to do so. You are affected by their impact upon your emotional bodies (not your minds) after these divine impulses have filtered through from the Shamballa and the hierarchical centres into and through the human centre and have then been seized upon and applied to specific national, racial and political conditions. You are hardly at all affected by the pure idealism which gave them birth and which lies behind them as the motivating (though unrecognised) impulse. You cannot grasp or view these great mental trends as does the Hierarchy. Hence much of your confusion and your difficulty.

If we consider these three great planetary centres and their relationships in tabular form we can get the general idea more clearly in mind:

I. SHAMBALLA .... Will or Power .... Planetary head centre,
   The Holy City ...... Purpose..Plan   spiritual pineal gland.
                        Life Aspect.
                Ruler:—Sanat Kumara, the Lord of the World.
                        The Ancient of Days.
                        Melchizedek.

II. THE HIERARCHY .... Love-Wisdom .... Planetary heart centre.
    The new Jerusalem... Consciousness.
                         Group unity.
                 Ruler:—The Christ.
                         The World Saviour.

III. HUMANITY .... Active Intelligence .... Planetary throat centre.
     The city, standing
        foursquare .... Self-consciousness.
                           Creativity.
                  Ruler:—Lucifer.
                          Son of the Morning.
                          The Prodigal Son.

These three centres are closely interrelated and must be thought of in their entirety as expressions of divine livingness, as embodying three great stages in the unfoldment of God's plan and as constituting the three major centres in the body of the "One in Whom we live and move and have our being." Students who have studied as you have can relate if they so choose, these three centres to the three solar systems, referred to in *A Treatise on Cosmic Fire*—

1. In the first solar system, the centre which is *Humanity*

was prepared, and the principle of intelligence came into manifestation.

2. In the second solar system, the *Hierarchy* of love made its appearance and must eventually come into full manifestation upon the physical plane, thereby enabling the Love of God to be seen.

3. In the next solar system, the centre which we today call *Shamballa* will manifest (intelligently and through love) the will aspect of Deity. It is only however in this *second* solar system that all these three centres, expressing the three divine aspects, meet simultaneously at various stages of livingness. It is interesting to note that it is only through human beings that these centres can ever come into true functioning activity.

Little is known of Shamballa except by Members of the Hierarchy to Whom that centre is the goal in the same way that the Hierarchy is, at this time, the goal for humanity. Shamballa is the directing centre for the Hierarchy. Little is really known of the will of God except by Those Whose function it is to interpret and express that will through love, intelligently applied. They know what the immediate purpose is and Their major occupation is the working out of that will into manifestation.

We have, therefore, three great centres and from them emanate three types of energy which are taking form as the three governing ideologies in the consciousness of the race. Old ideologies still persist; subsidiary schools of thought are everywhere to be found; distorted interpretations and travesties of reality abound on every hand; on all sides the dead level of the people (the ignorant masses) is played upon by these energies and men become victims of the exponents of the ideologies—past, present and future.

Forget not that behind all of them stands He Whom we call the Lord of the World. When all these temporary experiments have been tried and when humanity has been led on in its consciousness from one stage of understanding to another and of recognised interrelation, the kingdom of God will be established upon Earth and the Ruler of the Earth will then work through the Hierarchy to produce that synthetic living creative response from nature (of which humanity is a part) which will enable each kingdom fully to reveal the glory of God. Shamballa will work through the Hierarchy and the Hierarchy, in its turn, will reach the various kingdoms in nature through the medium of Humanity, which will then enter into its pre-ordained and destined function. It is for this that all is taking place. The time of fruition lies relatively far ahead but in the meantime humanity is experimenting or is the subject of experiment; it is exploiting or being exploited; it is learning the lessons of enforced obedience or the dangers of selfish license; it is victimised by powerful personalities in every land and this without exception, or it is being guided in right directions (and this again without exception) by the emissaries and disciples of either Shamballa or the Hierarchy. All vaunted freedom or vaunted control is but the temporary reaction of a humanity which is swept by ideas, controlled by ideals, impulsed by selfishness, impregnated by hates and yet all the time is struggling to express the higher and better qualities and to free itself from the thralldom of ancient evil, the slavery of ancient codes and the curse of ancient habits of thought and living. It is what is happening behind the scenes to mankind *as a whole* which is of moment; it is the unfoldment of the human consciousness which counts with the Hierarchy, and that unfolds in response to the presented conditions in any country or countries. Let me assure you that under the pressure of modern life, under the strain of the imposed present conditions and civilisation, plus the mental concern, the terror of marching armies, the thunder of the many voices and the stress of the worldwide economic stringency, the human consciousness is rapidly awakening from its long sleep. That great and fundamental reality which you call the "human state of mind" is just beginning to focus itself upon the things which matter and to express itself in a living fashion. That is the factor of moment and not the happenings in any particular country.

And, I would remind you, all that is occurring is an evidence of energy and is expressive of force. That is the factor never to be forgotten. It is essential that you recognise them as existing. There is little that you, as individuals or as groups, can do about them beyond seeing to it that there is nothing in you which could make you—unimportant as you may be—a focal point for hate, separation, fear, pride and other characteristics which feed the fires which threaten to bring disaster to the world. Each of you can aid more than you can guess through the regulation of thought and ideas, through the cultivation of a loving spirit and through the general use of the Great Invocation whereby these forces and energies—so sorely needed—can be invoked.

We have now considered the three major energies which are pouring into our planetary life at this time through the three major centres. It remains for us now to consider the energy of the two minor rays, the sixth and the seventh, which are in many ways of more *immediate* moment to the masses and of a tremendous effectiveness. One is of moment because of its pronounced hold and because of the crystallisation it has produced particularly in the world of thought, and the other because its hold and its power, its influence and its effects will be of an increasing momentum. One is potent in producing the necessity for the present chaos; the other is potential and holds in its activity the seeds of the future.

This is a fact of great interest and of really practical import. It takes us, moreover, into the realm of prevision. I would have you remember, at this point, that no prevision is divorced entirely from the past but that there must always be the seed of truth. The Law of Cause and Effect holds good eternally and particularly so in the realm of spiritual insight (so rapidly developing at this time) which enables the seer to see the future as it may be and to forecast coming eventualities. There are several ways in which such prevision can—during the next three centuries—be developed in the race of men:

1. Through the development of soul contact among the advanced members of the race. This contact will relate soul knowledge with brain impression and, if the meditating factor of the mind is duly trained and controlled, there will be a correct foreknowledge of individual destiny and of coming events.

2. Through the development of the science of astrology—a science which is, as yet, in its infancy and which is based on so many uncertain factors that it is difficult for a student to arrive at those true indications which will truly present the future. Character indications and small personality happenings can frequently and correctly be deduced but the general subject remains until today much too nebulous for certitude. I will later deal with this matter and will indicate the lines along which future investigation should proceed.

3. Through the recurrence of "soothsaying" and the reap-

pearance of those ancient "informers of the race" who, in Roman times, were called "sibyls." These mediums (for such they were) will be trained by the workers upon the seventh ray to speak under inspiration from the Hierarchy Whose foreknowledge extends far ahead into the future, but does not extend beyond two thousand years. These mediums will, however, only be used under direction, after careful training and only twice a year at the May and June Full Moon rituals.

As to the prevision with which I shall deal, unorthodox as it may appear to be to some of you, it will be based upon two factors: First of all, the logical indications to be gathered from past and present events which condition the immediate future and which must inevitably lead to definite and tangible happenings. Any deep student of human affairs could follow the same line of reasoning and come to approximately the same conclusions, *provided* he loved his fellowmen enough to see them truly as they were and allow, consequently, for the appearance of the unexpected. And, secondly, what I may say to you is based on a knowledge of the ray influences which are at this time so powerfully and effectively affecting humanity and its coming civilisation and culture.

I would ask you, therefore, to read what I have to say with an open mind; I would beg you to relate my words to present world conditions and to see, emerging from the realms of subjectivity, those forces and potencies which are directly changing the current of men's thoughts, which are moulding their ideas, and incidentally altering the face of the earth and the policies of nations.

As you know, there are at this time, two minor rays (which are rays of attribute) affecting powerfully the destiny of mankind. These are the sixth Ray of Abstract Devotion or Idealism and the seventh Ray of Ceremonial Magic or Organisation. The sixth ray began to pass out of manifestation in 1625 after a long period of influence, whilst the seventh Ray of Ceremonial Order began to come into manifestation in 1675. There are three points to be remembered in connection with these two rays and their effects upon the race of men. (I am not here dealing with their effects upon the other kingdoms in nature.)

1. The sixth ray is, as you know, the most powerful in manifestation in this time and a very large number of people are responsive to its influence. It is still the line of least resistance for the majority, particularly in the Aryan race, for the reason that when in process of time and through evolution the influence of a ray has become potent, it is groups that are primarily affected and not just individuals. A rhythm and a momentum is then set up which lasts a long time and which gains power through the very force of organised numbers. This truth will emerge more clearly as we proceed with our studies. Suffice it to say that the sixth ray people are the reactionaries, the conservatives, the die-hards and the fanatics, who hold on to all that is of the past and whose influence is potent to hinder the progress of humanity into the new age. Their name is legion. They provide, however, a needed balance and are responsible for a steadying process which is much needed in the world at this time.

2. The seventh ray is steadily gaining momentum and has for a long time been stimulating and enhancing the activity of all fifth ray nations. If you bear in mind that one of the major objectives of seventh ray energy is to bring

together and to relate spirit and matter and also substance and form (note this distinction) you can see
for yourself that the work of science is closely connected
with this endeavour and that the creation of the new
forms will definitely be the result of a working inter-
action between the rulers of the fifth, the second and
the seventh rays, aided by the help—on demand—of the
ruler of the first ray. A large number of seventh ray
egos or souls and also of men and women with seventh
ray personalities are coming into incarnation now, and
to them is committed the task of organising the activities of the new era and of ending the old methods of
life and the old crystallised attitudes to life, to death,
to leisure and to the population.

3. The result of the increasing flow of seventh ray energy
plus the decreasing influence of the sixth ray—which
shows itself as a pronounced crystallisation of the standardised and accepted forms of belief, religious, social
and philosophic—is to throw the millions of people who
do not respond to either of the above influences through
egoic or personality relation, into a state of bewilderment. They feel entirely lost, are gripped by the idea
that life holds for them no desirable future, all that
they have learnt to cherish and to hold dear is rapidly
failing.

These three groups of people, influenced by the sixth
and seventh rays or who are bewildered by the impact of
forces generated by those rays, are those who must together,
with understanding and clear vision, bring order out of the
present chaos. They must materialise those new and desirable conditions which will conform to the subjective pattern
in the minds of the illumined people of the world and to

the spiritual plan as it exists in the consciousness of the members of the Hierarchy. The new age with its peculiar civilisation and culture will be brought into manifestation through the collaboration of the well-intentioned many, responsive increasingly to the good of the whole and not of the individual; they are the idealistic but practical thinkers, influenced by the pattern of things to come and the world disciples, impressed by the plans and under the instruction of the Hierarchy which is directing and controlling all.

It is with these three groups of people and with the work upon which they are engaged that any prevision I may evidence will consistently deal. All changes in connection with the human family, the fourth kingdom in nature, are always dependent upon three factors:

1. Those outer physical events which are definitely "acts of God" and over which no human being has the slightest authority.

2. The activity of human beings themselves, working on all the different rays but in any given time and in any particular period conditioned by:

    a. The preponderance of egos to be found on any particular ray. There are a very large number of second ray egos in incarnation today and their work and their lives will facilitate the coming Great Approach.

    b. The nature and the quality of the predominating personality rays of the majority. At this time there are a vast number of souls in incarnation whose personality rays are either the sixth or the third. They condition the coming civilisation outstandingly including all educational and financial enterprises, just as the influence of those who have soul contact and can express soul quality condition and determine the current culture.

c. The activity of the fifth principle, that of the mind. This mind principle is peculiarly active today in a broad and general sense. If I might put it symbolically the *vertical activity* of the mind which has affected individuals everywhere down the ages has always produced the mental guides, the directors and the leaders of humanity. Today, the *horizontal activity* of the mind, embracing huge masses of the populace and sometimes entire nations and races, can everywhere be seen and this must lead inevitably to events and effects hitherto unvisioned and impossible.

3. The influence of the outgoing and the incoming rays at any time. You have often been told that these events —for the emergence or disappearance of a ray influence is an event in time—are a matter of slow development, are psychic in nature, and are governed by law. The length of time in which a ray appears, manifests and does its work and finally disappears is one of the secrets of initiation, but—as time elapses and the nature of time itself is better understood—the period and the time equation of the minor rays of attribute will be established but that time is not yet, although the intense interest taken today in the phenomena of time indicates a growing awareness of the problem itself and of the need for understanding the relation of time, both to space and to event. It will be realised before long that time is entirely a brain event; a study of the sense of speed as registered by the brain, plus the capacity or incapacity of a human being to express this speed, will, when properly approached, reveal much that today remains a mystery.

At this time, the whole world is embroiled in the chaos

and the turmoil incident upon the clashing of the forces of the sixth and the seventh rays. As one ray passes out and another comes into manifestation and their impact upon the earth and upon all the forms in all the kingdoms of nature has reached the point where the two influences are equalised, then a definite point of crisis is reached. This is what has occurred today, and humanity, subjected to two types or forms of energy, is thrown "off centre" and hence the intense difficulty and tension of the present world period. The cause of this is not only the impact of the two types of energy, beating upon the forms of life with equal force, but also that the energy of humanity itself (which is a combination of the fourth and fifth rays) is swept into the conflict. To this must also be added the energy of the animal kingdom (again a combination of the energies of the third, fifth and sixth rays) for this governs the animal or physical form of every human being. You have, therefore, a meeting of many conflicting forces and the world Arjuna is faced with a stupendous battle—one that is recurrent and cyclic but which will, in this particular era, prove a decisive and determining factor in the age old conflict between material domination and spiritual control. The forces playing upon the planet at this time are of supreme importance. If you will bear in mind that the sixth ray works through and controls the solar plexus (being closely related to the astral plane, the sixth level of awareness) and that the seventh ray controls the sacral centre, you will see why there is so much emotion, so much idealism and so much desire mixed up in connection with the world conflict and why also— apart from the storms in the political arena and the religious field—that sex and its various problems has reached a point of interest in the human consciousness where a solution of these difficulties, a fresh understanding of the underlying implications and a frank dealing with the situation is inevitable and immediate.

Four problems will be solved in the next two centuries:

1. The problem of territorial possessions which is the group correspondence within the family of nations to the materiality of the individual.

2. The problem of sex which will involve a truer understanding of the law of attraction.

3. The problem of death, which is in reality the problem of the relation between the subjective and the objective, between the tangible and the intangible, and between life and form. This problem will be solved in the realm of psychology by scientific recognition of the true nature of the individual or soul and of the persona.

4. The problem of the Jews which is symbolically the problem of humanity as a whole. It is today for the first time definitely a humanitarian problem and one which is closely tied up with the fourth kingdom in nature because that kingdom is the meeting-place of the three divine aspects. The Jew, with his emphasis upon his position as one of the "chosen people," has stood symbolically throughout the centuries as the representative of the wandering, incarnating soul, but the Jewish people have never recognised the symbolic mission with which their race was entrusted, and they have taken to themselves the glory and the honour of the Lord's elect. The Jew made this mistake and, as an Oriental race, the Jews have failed to hold before the Orient the divine nature of mankind as a whole, for all are equally divine and all are the Lord's elect. Calvin and all who followed his lead made the same mistake and instead of holding before the people of the Occident the realisation that those

who recognised their essential divinity did so symbolically on behalf of all the developing, incarnating sons of
God, they regarded themselves as the Chosen People
and all who did not think as they did are regarded as lost.
When the Jew and the narrow-minded religious devotees recognise their identity with all other people and
express this identity through right relationship, we shall
see a very different world. The world problem is essentially a religious problem and behind all strife in every
department of world thought today is to be found the
religious element.

When the nature of the present struggle is better understood and its subjective causes are considered instead of the
superficial objective reasons, then real progress will be
made in the process of releasing humanity from the thral-
dom and the narrowness of the present civilisation and from
the influence of the forces and energies which are responsible
for the situation. These will be understood, correctly han-
dled and rightly directed towards constructive and desirable
ends. In the realm of this conflict, the great and fundamental law that "energy follows thought" always holds
good, and one of the conditions which is inducing the present
stress and strain is due to the fact that so many millions of
people are beginning to think. This means that the ancient
simplicity which has held good up to five hundred years ago
is no longer controlling and the situation is much more complex. In ancient days the forces were largely controlled by
the Lords of Materiality (those whom the ignorant and the
prejudiced esotericist call "the black forces"); the forces of
spirituality plus the thought of a handful of advanced men
in the different nations were not so potent as they are today.
The situation was then relatively simple. It was part of the

evolutionary plan that matter and substance should temporarily control and that spirit should learn to "mount on the shoulders of matter" as the Ancient Wisdom puts it. Now, however, owing to the widespread education of the masses and the many means of worldwide propaganda, these masses are themselves either thinking independently or are thinking as directed by the powerful minds everywhere to be found and which are seeking to control world events. Hence the increasing difficulty of the problem and one that is equally difficult for the Lords of the Left Hand Way as it is for the Great White Lodge. This is a point which you should consider and discover the implications.

Humanity itself is rapidly arriving at the point where its *united will* will be the determining factor in world affairs and this will be due to the unfoldment of the mind through the success of the evolutionary process. It is right here that many experiments will be made (and are being made today) and many mistakes must inevitably take place. The major requirement therefore at this time is the rapid educating of the people in the Plan and in the nature of the forces which are controlling evolution and their directing agencies. The fact of the Hierarchy must be announced in no uncertain terms, thereby arousing public interest, public investigation and public recognition. In the process of so doing much will be learnt of the balancing group of initiates and adepts who work entirely with the material side of life and in whom (for this major world cycle) the love aspect of the soul remains totally undeveloped, whereas the mind nature is potently expressing itself. If you will study what I have earlier given anent certain of the higher and lower expressions of the rays you will see how these two fields of endeavour—that of the Hierarchy, animated by love and that of the opposite pole, the Black Lodge, working entirely through mind and substance—are engaged and their close relationship will emerge. You will realise then that the margin of difference is very slight and is to be found solely *in intention,* in the underlying purpose and the concrete objectives which this group of material workers have set themselves. The major instrument of the Black Lodge is the organising power of the mind and not the coherent influence of love, as is the case with the Masters of the Wisdom. Yet in the natural process of form evolution, these workers on the darker side of life have their useful function. Because they are working predominantly through the mental principle, we find the susceptibility of the untrained masses to this mental imposition and the facility with which they can be regimented and standardised. They have no power to think with clarity for themselves and their minds are consequently plastic and receptive to the powerful forces directed by the two contributing groups—the spiritual workers of the planet and the material workers. Because the bulk of human beings are still materially focussed, the forces which work on the side of matter find a line of least resistance which is not available to the Masters of the Great White Lodge. This danger is, however, lessening decade by decade.

Let me illustrate these facts for you by means of the two rays which are our immediate consideration. Both of them—as is ever the law—express themselves through a higher and lower form or forms. One of the higher expressions of the out-going sixth ray is to be found in Christianity, the spirit and principles of which were embodied for us in the life of the Master Jesus, Who was, in His turn, inspired and over-shadowed and used by His great Ideal, the Christ. In the word "idealism" you have the keynote of this ray—idealism taking form, providing a living example and indicating to the race of men their own divine potentialities. In the appearance of the Christ, the divine ideal for the race, as a whole, was presented for the first time. Other and earlier Sons of God presented diverse divine qualities and attributes, but in three of them a certain perfection of presentation was achieved which (as far as this present world period is concerned) can never be surpassed.

These three are: Hercules, the perfect disciple but not yet the perfected Son of God; the Buddha, the perfect initiate, having reached illumination but not yet having developed to perfection all the attributes of divinity; the Christ, the absolutely perfect expression of divinity for this cycle and, therefore, the Teacher alike of angels and of men. That ahead of the race may lie a still higher perfection than that attained by any of these Exponents of divinity is inexpressibly true, for we know not yet what divinity really means; in these three, however, we have three instances of a perfection which lies far ahead for the majority of the sons of men.

In all of Them, the sixth and the second rays were controlling factors, with the first ray reaching full expression. In Them, idealism, love-wisdom and indomitable will stood forth in all their divine power. It might be of interest to you to know just what rays controlled these Sons of God:

Hercules, the Sun-God, had a first ray soul, a second ray personality and a sixth ray astral body. These potencies and energies sufficed to carry Him through all the trials and the labours of the disciple.

The Buddha had a second ray soul, a first ray personality and a sixth ray mind—a very rare phenomenon.

The Christ had a second ray soul, a sixth ray personality (which accounted for His close relationship with the Master Jesus), plus a first ray mind.

These three all embodied the essences of the spiritual life and all of Them were enabled to set Their seal upon history and upon the hearts of men, largely through the potency of Their sixth ray expression. All of Them embodied also the new spiritual impulse which Their day and age required and all of Them for centuries—by the strength of Their living love and power—brought the vision and the aspiration of humanity back to those spiritual essentials whereby men must live. All of Them were part of the directing group of Lives Who are working out the plans of God, founded upon the love of God. The Buddha and the Christ are still closely connected with, and working in cooperation with, the Hierarchy. Hercules has gone over into the Shamballa centre, but still works in a basic association with the Buddha Who is one of the Forces linking Shamballa and the Hierarchy.

Pure religion, undefiled and spiritually focussed, is the higher expression of the sixth ray (working as is ever the case under the influence and potency of the second ray) and for us Christianity in its earlier days was the great and inspiring symbol.

In the same connection, among the *lower aspects* of the sixth ray are to be found all forms of dogmatic, authoritative religion as expressed by the organised and orthodox churches. All formulated theologies are the lower expression of the higher spiritual truths because they embody the mind reactions of the religious man, his confidence in his own personal mind deductions and the surety that he is obviously right. They do not embody the spiritual values as they truly exist. Consequently the dreadful nature of the lower expressions of the sixth ray and the control by the forces of separativeness (which are ever the outstanding characteristic of the lower sixth ray activity) can be seen nowhere more potently than in religious and Church history with its hatreds and bigotry, its pomp and luxurious appeal to the outer ear and eye, and its separativeness from all other forms of faith as well as its internal dissensions, its protesting groups and its cliques and cabals. The Church has wandered far from the simplicity which is in Christ. Theologians have lost (if they ever possessed it) the "mind that is in Christ" and the outstanding need of the Church today is to relinquish theology, to let go all doctrine and dogma and to turn upon the world the light that is in Christ, and thus demonstrate the fact of Christ's eternal livingness, and the beauty and the love which it can reflect from its contact with Him, the founder of Christianity but not of Churchianity.

I generalise. There are those in the Church today who do express all that I have stated and who are reflections in the truest sense of the living Christ. They relegate theology and authority to their rightful place and regard the discussions of theologians as simply expressions of perhaps needed mental gymnastics and as incentives to thought, but they do not regard them as conditioning factors, determining man's salvation or not. They know that man's salvation is determined by the processes of evolution and is not a question of ultimate achievement but simply one of time; they know that the life within a man will bring him ultimately to his goal and that the experiences and the type of incarnation will inevitably lead him to "his desired haven." His salvation is not determined by his acceptance of some dogma, formulated by men who have lost their sense of proportion (and consequently their sense of humor) and who deem themselves capable of interpreting the mind of God for their fellowmen.

It should be here remembered that there are divine attributes and ray characteristics which have hitherto never been revealed to the minds of men or sensed by them in their highest moments of inspiration; this is due to the lack of sensitivity of even the most advanced of the sons of men. Their apparatus remains inadequately developed and so unable to respond to these higher divine qualities. Even the Christ Himself and other Members of the Great White Lodge are preparing Themselves to register these divine attributes and consciously to merge Themselves in a still higher process or scale of evolution; it will be obvious to you that the little conclusions of the little minds are some of the most dangerous factors today in world affairs.

It will also be apparent to you how the lower and the higher expressions of a ray are closely related to each other and how easily the higher loses its hold and the lower comes into manifestation—something that evolution itself must eventually adjust.

It is harder to differentiate between the higher and the lower expressions of the seventh Ray of Ceremonial Order, for this ray is only in process of manifestation and we know not as yet what its major expressions will be, either higher or lower. Human reactions have their place and—as I have earlier pointed out—even the Masters Themselves do not and cannot foretell what the results of the impacts of force may be nor what may eventuate as a result, though They can frequently determine the probable happenings. If I say to you that the higher expression of the seventh ray is white magic, do you really understand what I mean? I question it. Have you any true idea of what is intended by these two words? I doubt it. White magic is realistically the power of the trained worker and executive to bring together into a constructive synthesis the "within and the without" so that that which is below may be recognisably patterned upon that which is above. It is the supreme task of bringing together in accordance with the immediate intent and plan and for the benefit of the evolving life in any particular world cycle:

1. Spirit and matter.
2. Life and form.
3. The ego and the personality.
4. The soul and its outer expression.
5. The higher worlds of atma—buddhi—manas and the lower reflection of mind—emotion and the physical nature.
6. The head and the heart, through the sublimation of the sacral and the solar plexus energies.
7. The etheric-astral planes and the dense physical plane.
8. The intangible subjective levels of existence and the outer tangible worlds.

Such is the task of the white magician and as evolution proceeds and becomes more complicated and complex it will nevertheless be more rapid and more accurately defined in the mind of the magician. All, therefore, that is conducive to human sensitivity and to increased awareness is the work of the white magician; all that tends to produce better forms through which the living principle of deity can express itself is the work of the white magician; all that serves to thin or tear away the veil between the worlds wherein those who have no physical bodies live and move and work and the worlds of outer form is the work of the white magician. Of all this type of work there is always much, but never more so than at this time owing to the coming into manifestation of this ray of the magician (black and white), the seventh ray. Hence the rapid growth of the sense of omnipresence and the recognition of the non-existence of time in relation to reality. This has taken place through the discovery and use of the radio and of the many means of communication and through the steady growth of telepathic interplay; hence also the spread of education, enlarging man's horizon and opening up to him new worlds for investigation and adventure; hence also the breaking down of the old and limiting forms through the invoked force of the first ray, which has hitherto always worked through the medium of the seventh ray, because the kingdoms in nature cannot yet stand pure first ray energy; hence also the keen interest in the life after death and the appearance of all the many groups which are today investigating the nature of survival and the probability of immortality; hence again the appearance of the modern spiritualistic movement. This is a direct effect of the coming into manifestation of the seventh ray. Spiritualism was the religion of old Atlantis and the seventh ray dominated that ancient civilisation for a very long period of time, particularly during the first half of its existence, just as the fifth ray is of such dominant potency in our Aryan age and race.

It is through the correct development of spiritualism along psychological lines and the withdrawal of its emphasis upon phenomena (which is its outstanding characteristic and emphasis today) that the true nature of death and of the hereafter will be revealed. But it is in connection with spiritualism that I can best illustrate the lower expression of the incoming seventh ray influences. The work of the seventh ray is, as you know, the relating of life and of form, but when the emphasis is laid upon the form aspect then the wrong procedure eventuates and the work of the black magician can begin, and his objectives come unduly into play. This is what has happened in the spiritualistic movement; its investigators are occupied with the form side of life and its adherents with the satisfaction of their emotional desires (again related to the form side) so that the true import of the movement is in danger of being lost.

Spiritualism, in its lowest and material aspect, is a low grade expression of the seventh ray and is—for the masses—definitely a line of least resistance, and, therefore, of no great spiritual importance to their evolutionary development. The masses of the people are today Atlantean in their consciousness and are only slowly emerging into the Aryan point of view. This must change and the mind activity be rapidly enhanced or else true spiritualism will be unable to express itself and—through the present spiritualistic movement—there can be let loose upon the world forces and entities of a most undesirable character. The negativity of the majority of those who are interested in spiritualism and the entire negativity of the bulk of the mediums throws the door wide open to very definite dangers. Fortunately, there is a movement within spiritualistic circles to right this obvious danger and to shift the present emphasis upon phenomena into the world of true values and right understanding. The subject is too vast a one for me to deal with here, except in illustration of the points which I am endeavouring to make, but one hint I will give. If the societies and organisations, connected with the spiritualistic movement and the psychical research groups, would seek for and find the natural sensitives (and not the trance mediums) and those who are naturally clair-audient and clair-voyant and would study their disclosures, their words, their reactions and their modes of working they would discover much about some of the natural and normal powers of man—powers which have been in abeyance during the period wherein mind development has been the objective and which humanity shares with two great groups of lives—the Members of the Hierarchy and the animal kingdom. Ponder on this. If, therefore, these societies would concentrate on the *intelligent and mental psychics* and rule out all trance conditions it would not be long before revelation would come. The trance condition is undesirable, separates the medium from his soul and definitely relegates him to the realm of the negative, of the uncontrolled and of material forces. This development, however, the forces of materiality will prevent if possible because the moment there is positive intelligent understanding of the world on the other side of the veil, there is no fear of death and then the major aspect of their power and of their hold upon humanity will disappear.

If you have followed intelligently what I have said, two points will emerge with clarity in your minds in relation to the initial and immediate activity of these two rays—the sixth and the seventh. First, that entire groups of people are increasingly susceptible to their influence and this inevitably leads to these groups (responsive to either the sixth or the seventh ray forces) being in opposition to and antagonistic to each other. The problem is that, owing to the developed sensitivity of the race, this antagonism is now upon a world-wide scale. Hence much of the present conflict of ideas, and the opposing ideologies, and hence also the feud between the old inherited traditions and the ancient forms of civilisation, of government, of religion on the one hand and of the newer emerging ideas on the other. These new concepts should usher in the New Age and will eventually revolutionise our modern life and standards. They will relegate the old ideas to the same position as the ideas which governed the race one thousand years ago have today assumed in our consciousness.

Second: The situation is still further complicated by

the fact that both these rays influence and express themselves (as is ever the case) in a dual manner and have always a lower and a higher form of manifestation, which
is a correspondence in this connection to the personality,
and the egoic expression of every human being. In the case
of the out-going ray, the higher form (which is ever the first
to manifest in germ) is rapidly disappearing or is being absorbed into the newer idealism, thus contributing all that
is best to the new presentation of truth so that the emerging
culture will be properly rooted in the old. The lower forms
are, however, tenacious and dominant and because of this
they definitely constitute today the major problem of the
Hierarchy, so much so that they require the calling in of
the first ray (or the Shamballa force) in order to effect their
destruction. Bear this in mind as you study the world situation. The lower forms of the seventh ray expression are
still in an embryonic stage. This you can see clearly if you
consider the one to which I chose to refer—the spiritualistic
movement—which began to take shape only during the last
century and has achieved its curiously phenomenal growth
only because it started upon the American continent. The
United States of America was the centre of old Atlantis and
hence inherited a psychic and ancient religious form which
was existent and potently alive in that part of the world
for many centuries.

In spite of these facts, the higher and more living energy
of the seventh ray is the most active at this time and its resultant idealism and consequent New Age concepts are playing upon the sensitive minds of the race and preparing humanity for a great and much needed change. The work of
the Ray of Ceremonial Order is to "ground" or make
physically visible the results of bringing spirit and matter

together. Its function is to clothe spirit with matter, producing form.

2. *The Nations and the Rays.*

In connection with this discussion which governs and influences the leading nations of the world, the student should bear in mind the fact that all are today primarily conditioned by the Law of Cleavages; however, advanced groups in every nation are beginning to respond to the Law of Understanding. This is a law which will eventually emphasise the eternal brotherhood of man and the identity of all souls with the Oversoul. This will be recognised in the racial consciousness, as well as the oneness of the Life which pours through, permeates, animates and integrates the entire solar system. This Life functions in and through all planetary schemes, in all their kingdoms of forms and with all that can be included under the phrase "form life." That phrase contains three basic ideas: the ideas of life, of form and of evolution.

The functioning of the Law of Loving Understanding will be greatly facilitated and speeded during the Aquarian Age which we are considering; it will eventuate later in the development of a world-wide international spirit, in the recognition of one universal faith in God and in humanity also as the major expression of divinity upon the planet and in the transfer of the human consciousness from the world of material things to that of the more purely psychic. This will lead in time and inevitably to the world of spiritual realities. It should be remembered that (for advanced humanity) the sequence of the recognition of these expansions of consciousness is as follows:

1. The world of psychical living. This requires the recognition, by the brain consciousness, of the need for mental

and spiritual control, as the first step.

2. The world of mental unfoldment.
3. The world of the soul or ego, the individualised man. When these recognitions are established in the aspirant, then there comes the recognition by the disciple of the Master Who should guide him.
4. The control of the physical plane life by the soul.
5. The functioning and the utilisation of the psychic powers and their place and part in the field of intelligent service.
6. The interpretative faculty of the illumined mind.
7. An inspired creative life upon the physical plane.

In that development of the racial consciousness, the process does not necessarily follow the above seven stages and sequence. This is owing to the stimulation and consequent sensitising of the form aspect through the increased radiation and potency of the dynamic New Group of World Servers; their ranks are filled by those who have passed, or are passing, through the stages of aspirant and disciple, thus learning to serve. Psychic unfoldment in the masses parallels the spiritual unfoldment of advanced humanity. This can be seen going on today on a large scale everywhere and it accounts for the tremendous growth of the spiritualistic movement and for the enormous increase in the lower psychic powers. Old Atlantean magic and the lower psychism are upon us again in the great turning of the wheel of life, but this time good may eventuate, if the world disciples and the spiritually-minded people measure up to their opportunity.

Today there are many thousands coming under the influence of this Law of Loving Understanding. Many in every nation are responding to the broader synthetic brotherly note, but the masses as yet understand nothing of this. They must be led in right ways gradually by the steady development in right understanding of their own nationals. Bear this in mind, all of you who work for world peace and right human relations, for harmony and for synthesis.

All of the great nations are controlled by two rays, just as is the human being. With the smaller nations we need not concern ourselves. All the nations are controlled by a personality ray, which is the dominant potent and main controlling factor at this time, and by a soul ray which is sensed only by the disciples and the aspirants of any nation.

This soul ray must be evoked into an increased functioning activity by the New Group of World Servers, for this is one of their main objectives and tasks. This must never be lost to sight. Much could be written about the historical influence of the rays during the past two thousand years and of the way in which great events have been influenced or brought about by the periodic ray influence. Interesting as it is and indicative of the present national trends and problems, all that I can now do is to point out the energies governing each nation, and leave you to study and note their effect and to comprehend their relation to the present condition of the world. One thing I would point out and that is that those rays which govern a particular nation and which are at this time actively working are very potent, either materially or egoically; some of the problems may be due to the fact that certain rays, governing certain nations, are not at this time active.

A close analysis of the following will reveal certain lines of racial understanding. There is a natural rapport indicated between the present personality rays of Germany and Great Britain, yet a relationship can be seen also between France and Great Britain through their esoteric national

Nation	Personality Ray	Soul Ray	National Motto
India	4th Ray, Harmony through Conflict.	1st Ray of Power	I hide the Light.
China	3rd Ray of Intelligence	1st Ray of Power	I indicate the Way.
Germany	1st Ray of Power	4th Ray of Harmony through Conflict.	I preserve.
France	3rd Ray of Intelligence	5th Ray of Knowledge	I release the Light.
Great Britain	1st Ray of Power	2nd Ray of Love	I serve.
Italy	4th Ray of Harmony through Conflict.	6th Ray of Idealism	I carve the Paths.
U. S. A.	6th Ray of Idealism	2nd Ray of Love	I light the Way.
Russia	6th Ray of Idealism	7th Ray of Order	I link two Ways.
Austria	5th Ray of Knowledge	4th Ray of Harmony through Conflict.	I serve the lighted Way.
Spain	7th Ray of Order	6th Ray of Idealism	I disperse the Clouds.
Brazil	2nd Ray of Love	4th Ray of Harmony through Conflict.	I hide the seed.

mottoes and also between the two symbols which are also theirs. The symbol for France is the fleur de lys, which she adopted centuries ago under divine guidance, which symbol stands for the three divine aspects in manifestation. The symbol for Great Britain, under the same divine apportioning, is the three feathers, carried as the arms of the Prince of Wales. The scintillating and brilliant French intellect with its scientific bent is accounted for by the interplay of the third Ray of Active Intelligence with the fifth Ray of Scientific Understanding. Hence their amazing contribution to the knowledge and the thought of the world and their brilliant and colourful history. Be it remembered also that the glory of the empire which was France is but the guarantee of a glory of divine revelation which lies ahead in the future; it will never be theirs until they cease living in the wonder of their past and go forth into the future to demonstrate the fact of illumination which is the goal of all mental effort. When the intellect of the French is turned towards the discovery and the elucidation of the things of the spirit, then they will carry revelation to the world. When their egoic ray dominates the third ray and when the separative action of the fifth ray is transmuted into the revealing function of this ray, then France will enter into a period of new glory. Her empire will then be of the mind and her glory of the soul.

It is obvious that the governing faculty of the Ray of Will or Power is the outstanding characteristic of Great Britain. England is an exponent of the art of control and her function has been to produce the first tentative grouping of federated nations the world has seen and to demonstrate the possibility of such a grouping. The United States is doing a somewhat similar thing and is fusing the nationals of many nations into one federated state with many subsidiary states, instead of subsidiary nations. These two powers function in this way and with this wide objective in order eventually to give to the planet a system of groupings within one national border or empire, and yet with an international implication which will be symbolic of the coming new age technique of government. The second Ray of Love or of Attraction governs—from the soul angle—the British Empire and there is a relation between this fact and the fact that the astrological sign Gemini governs both the United States and London. The fluid, mercurial, intuitional mind is closely allied with the divine aspect of love and understanding, producing attraction and interpretation.

It is interesting to note that the fourth Ray of Harmony through Conflict which before long will come into power again, is to be prominent in the destinies of India, Germany, Italy, Austria and Brazil. It is for this that there is so much preparatory turmoil in four of these countries. The sixth Ray of Idealism is potent in Russia, the United States, Italy and Spain. It is the fanatical adherence to an ideal which is responsible for the potent changes in these four countries. In Germany and Italy the harmonising of the fourth ray, working through conflict, is also to be seen. Hence we have in all these countries a process of "breaking-down" and of destruction of old forms prior to an adequate responsiveness to the influence of the incoming ray. It should be remembered that as with individuals, so with nations—the reaction to an increasing influence of the soul ray is ever accompanied by a breaking down period; this demonstration of destruction is, however, only temporary and preparatory.

India hides the light and that light, when released upon the world and revealed to humanity, will bring about harmony in the form aspect; things will then be clearly seen as they are and will be freed from glamour and illusion; this harmonising light is sorely needed in India itself and when it has been manifested it will bring about the right functioning of the first Ray of Power or Government. The will of the people will then be seen in the light. It is in this connection that Great Britain will emerge into renewed activity for her personality ray and India's soul ray are the same. Many British people are subjectively linked with India, by past incarnations and association; the quarrel between Great Britain and India is largely a family affair in the deepest sense of the term and hence its bitterness. As you know, there is a close link between the fourth and second rays and this again emerges in the relationship between England and India; a destiny is there which must be jointly worked out.

The static stabilising tendency of Germany showed for instance in her futile effort to preserve a racial purity now, as then, impossible. This static quality is due to her first ray personality; her fourth ray energy was responsible for her effort to standardise and harmonise all the elements within her borders to the point of regimentation. This has been the line of least resistance for Germany, for though the first ray is not in manifestation at this time, yet the bulk of the people in power in Germany during the past world war (1914-1945) were all on the first subray of the seven rays and hence they were inevitably the transmitters of first ray energy. It is for this reason that Great Britain can contact the German race and handle the people in that sad country more understandingly than can the other nations or Great Powers. They share similar qualities and one of the services which Great Britain can render at this time is to come to the aid of world peace and live up to her motto, "I serve," by acting as an interpreter.

A careful analysis of the idealism of Russia and of the
United States may reveal no resemblances in the goal of
their idealism; the Russian is driven by his seventh ray
soul towards the imposition of an enforced ceremonial of
ordered rhythms, leading to an idealised order and a community of interests. Because of this and because of the
enforced work, some forces are present and active in Russia
which need most careful handling by the spiritual Hierarchy
of our planet. These forces working in Russia are concerned with the magic of form whereas pure white magic is
concerned only with the soul or with the subjective aspect,
as it conditions the objective. The "black forces," so
called, are nowhere rampant in Russia any more than in
other parts of the world, but the Russian reaction and
attitude to enforced rule and order has in it more of the
magical seventh ray influence than is the case in other
countries; Germany also enforced a standardised order
and way of living but this was definitely submitted to the
control of the black forces.

You will note that of the major nations only Brazil,
Great Britain and the United States of America are
definitely under the influence of the second Ray of Love-
Wisdom. An interesting fact thus emerges: Great Britain
is the custodian of the wisdom aspect of this second ray
energy for the Aryan race; the United States will fulfil
the same office for the world of the immediate future,
whilst Brazil will eventually—many thousands of years
hence—supersede both of them. These three races embody
the attractive cohesive aspect of the second ray and will
demonstrate it through wisdom and right government,
based on true idealism and love.

Great Britain represents that aspect of the mind which
expresses itself in intelligent government, based on just

and loving understanding. That is, of course, the ideal before her, but not as yet the exactly fulfilled achievement. The United States represents the intuitive faculty, expressing itself as illumination, plus the power to fuse and blend. Brazil will—at some distant date—represent a linking interpreting civilisation, based on the unfoldment of the abstract consciousness which is a blend of the intellect and the intuition and which serves to reveal the wisdom aspect of love in its beauty.

It is too dangerous in these days of difficulty and world turmoil to express myself more definitely as to the future lines of unfoldment. The destiny and the future functioning of the nations lie hid in their present activities. The majority of my readers are far too nationalistic in their thinking, and too deeply engrossed with the prime importance of their own nation and its supreme significance, for me to be able to do more than generalise and indicate the major lines of progress. The role of the prophet is a dangerous one, for destiny lies in the hands of the people and no one knows exactly what the people will do—once aroused and educated. The time has not yet come when the bulk of the people of any nation can see the picture whole or be permitted to know the exact part their nation must play in the history of nations. Every nation—without exception—has its peculiar virtues and vices which are dependent upon the point in evolution, the measure of control of the personality ray, the emerging control of the soul ray, and the general focus of the nation.

It is useful to bear in mind that some nations are negative and feminine and others are masculine and positive. India, France, the United States of America, Russia and Brazil are all feminine and constitute the nurturing mother aspect. They are feminine in their psychology—

intuitive, mystical, alluring, beautiful, fond of display and colour, and with the faults also of the feminine aspect, such as over emphasis upon the material aspects of life, upon pageantry, upon possession and upon money or its equivalent as a symbol of the form side of existence. They mother and nurture civilisation and ideas.

China, Germany, Great Britain and Italy are masculine and positive; they are mental, political, governing, standardising, group-conscious, occult by inclination, aggressive, full of grandeur, interested in law and in laying the emphasis upon race and empire. But they are more inclusive and think in wider terms than the feminine aspects of divine manifestation.

National relationships and the major intellectual cleavages are based also upon the governing ray influences. Spain, Austria and France, being governed by the seventh, fifth and third rays, have a close inter-relation. This worked out in a most interesting manner in the Middle Ages, and the destinies of these three nations were closely related. The newly forming country of the United States is likewise spiritually and intimately associated—in its form aspect—with Brazil, Russia and Italy; hence the early influx of certain types of emigrants into the country and hence also the pull of the South American countries upon the American consciousness, and the growth (rightly or wrongly) of the ideal of Pan-America. These relations are all on the form side and emerge out of the personality rays or energy of the nations concerned. The Ray of Love or Inclusiveness, the Ray of Active Intelligence showing itself so predominantly in the electrical civilisation of modern times, and the fifth Ray of Exact Science are all potently active at this time, for they are all pouring their energies onto our planetary life. The incoming seventh

Ray of Order is surely, even if slowly, imposing order and a new rhythm of life upon mankind. The effect of these incoming energies and of the rays which are active at any one time is felt in the following sequential order:

1. The sensing of an ideal.
2. The formulation of a theory.
3. The growth of public opinion.
4. The imposition of the new and developing pattern upon the evolving life.
5. The production of a form, based upon that pattern.
6. The stabilised functioning of the life within the new form.

It should be remembered that each ray embodies an idea which can be sensed as an ideal. The rays in time produce the world pattern which moulds all planetary forms and thus bears witness to the inner potency of the evolutionary processes. This pattern-forming tendency is being recognised today by modern psychology in connection with the human being and his emotional or thought patterns are being charted and studied. *So it is with the nations and races also.* Every ray produces three major patterns which are imposed upon the form nature, whether it be that of a man, a nation or a planet. These three patterns are: *the emotional pattern,* embodying the aspiration of a man, a nation or a race; it is the sumtotal of the desire tendency at any one time; *the mental pattern,* emerging later in time and governing the thought processes of a man, a nation or a race. The emotional and mental patterns are the negative and positive aspects of the personality of a man, a nation or a race. *The soul pattern* is the pre-disposing and spiritual goal, the ring-pass-not or destiny which the spiritual principle succeeds eventually in imposing upon the personality of a man, a nation or a race. This soul pattern eventually supersedes and obliterates the two earlier pattern-producing processes.

If, for instance, the energy of the fifth ray, which is the soul ray of the French nation, can make its potency felt in the stress and misery of the present world condition, then to France may be given the ultimate glory of proving to the world the fact of the soul and of giving a demonstration of soul control. The soul pattern may be translated by the genius of the French intellect into terms which humanity can understand and a true psychology of the soul may come into being. The genius of Germany has often in the past been expressed along the line of its fourth ray soul, and through its power Germany has given much of music and philosophy to mankind. That soul is not at present expressing itself; a rampant personality has expressed the greatest evil, but as time goes on and Germany learns the lessons which she must learn, the soul pattern will again be impressed upon the German consciousness; Germany must be helped to get again the vision of this ideal. If England's ideal of justice (which is the pattern of its personality ray) can be transformed by her soul ray of love into just and intelligent world service, then she will give to the world the pattern of that true government which is the genius of the soul quality of the British. If the idealism of the United States of America can be illumined by the law of love and not by personality self-expression, then the pattern which underlies the structure of the States may be seen in lines of light and we shall look for future racial light instead of the many separative national lines. At present it is the personality ray of the United States which controls.

A close study of that for which each nation stands will be most revealing and their pattern will emerge—a pattern of personality selfishness or a pattern of soul goals.

Italy has a sixth ray soul and hence her devotion to her past and to the ancient "glory which was Rome" (for this is closely tied up with the memory aspect of the soul) and to the concept of the restoration of the Roman Empire. But as it is the soul ray which is upon this stream of ray influence, it is interesting to note that Italy carries forward her plans with very little hate and with the minimum of persecution and of resentment; she stands steadily for peace, no matter what the people may believe under the influence of national propaganda and the theories of the newspapers. Her motto, esoterically stated, is, as you know: "I carve the Paths." This will be true eventually in the spiritual as well as in the literal sense. Rome was the great road builder and road maker of Europe in the far distant past; today the British race (who are largely re-incarnated Romans and hence the friendly feeling which basically exists between the two countries in spite of outer appearance) are the original railroad makers. This is all upon the material side. Upon the spiritual side, as I told you in an earlier book, the whole field of religion will be re-inspired and re-oriented from Rome because the Master Jesus will again take hold of the Christian Church in an effort to re-spiritualise it and to re-organise it. From the chair of the Pope of Rome, the Master Jesus will attempt to swing that great branch of the religious beliefs of the world again into a position of spiritual power and away from its present authoritative and temporary political potency.

The United States of America has for its personality ray the sixth ray and hence much of its personality difficulties. Hence also its strong desire life, impelling it to sex expression and to materiality but to a materiality which is very different from that of the French, for the citizen of the United States values money only for the effects on his life which it can bring and for what it makes possible. Hence also the rapid response of the American continent to every form of idealism, to the need of others, even of its enemies, to compassion for all suffering and to a pronounced progress towards a well defined humanitarianism. This they may call the democratic ideal but it is in truth something which grows out of and eventually supersedes democracy—the ideal of spiritual government—a government by the highest and the most spiritual to be found in the land. Hence also their unrealised esoteric motto: "I light the Way." All the various forms of government, prevalent in the world today, will—after making their great experiment and its resultant contribution—proceed upon the way of enlightened rule by the illumined minds of the age. This development is certain and inevitable and the indications of this happening can be seen today by those who have eyes to see and a developed inner vision.

Russia is peculiarly interesting at this time from the angle of humanity because she comes under the influence of both rays. Her egoic ray is the seventh and her personality ray is the sixth. Hence the tremendous conflict which is going on between the fanatical sixth ray cruelty of her sixth ray regime and the spiritual harmlessness which is the basic principle of the national ideology. Hence also the materiality of several important sections of her populace and the essential brotherliness which is imposed by the idealism and the mystical aspiration of the Russian genius, expressed through its people as a whole. Hence also the correctness of their spiritual motto which is as yet unrealised by them but which is working itself out noticeably to those of us who can see upon the inner side of life. That motto is: "I link two ways." Their task, which will develop as they come to truer understanding, is the linking of the East and of the West, and also of the worlds of desire and of spiritual aspiration, of the fanaticism which produces cruelty and the understanding which produces love, of a developed materialism and a perfected holiness, of the selfishness of a materialistic regime and the unselfishness of a mystically and spiritually minded people, and all this in a most pronounced and peculiar manner. Behind the closed borders of that mysterious and magnificent country, a great and spiritual conflict is proceeding and the rare mystical spirit and the truly religious orientation of the people is the eternal guarantee that a true and living religion and culture will finally emerge. Out of Russia—a symbol of the world Arjuna in a very special sense—will emerge that new and magical religion about which I have so often told you. It will be the product of the great and imminent Approach which will take place between humanity and the Hierarchy. From these two centres of spiritual force, in which the light which ever shineth in and from the East will irradiate the West, the whole world will be flooded with the radiance of the Sun of Righteousness. I am not here referring (in connection with Russia) to the imposition of any political ideology, but to the appearance of a great and spiritual religion which will justify the crucifixion of a great nation and which will demonstrate itself and be focussed in a great and spiritual Light which will be held aloft by a vital Russian exponent of true religion—that man for whom many Russians have been looking and who will be the justification of a most ancient prophecy.

Spain has a sixth ray ego and a seventh ray personality —thus reversing the forces which are expressing themselves through the Russian spirit. Spain, too, acts as a link in world adjustment but this time the link is between Europe and Africa, and in this capacity Spain has earlier served. It will be apparent to you also how inevitable has been the relationship between Spain and Russia and how the ideology of the latter country has influenced the national government. It will also be apparent why the battleground of two great ideologies—the Fascist and the Communistic—has been found inevitably in Spain. The triumph of the Fascist part has been equally inevitable from the start because of the egoic relation existing between Spain and Italy and also to the proximity of the two countries which has enabled the telepathic impress of Fascist idealism to be easily impressed upon the prepared and sensitive Spanish consciousness. As to the fanaticism, the natural cruelty, the fervent idealism, the arrogant pride and the religious and mystical quality of the Spanish character, they are obviously of sixth ray origin and are highly crystallised. The intense individualism of the people can be noted also as a definite part of their seventh ray personality equipment. Their spiritual motto: "I disperse the clouds," is indicative of the magical work for which Spain will eventually be responsible and sooner than is perhaps anticipated, thus balancing in that highly intelligent and individualistic country the field of scientific magic and the magical work of the Church of the future. This is a prophecy which lies at present too far ahead to be capable of verification, either in this generation or the next, but it is rooted in national characteristics and the law of probability.

We have been considering the rays of the Great Powers and the two Axis Powers, Germany and Italy. But the same methods can be applied to any nation and race and should prove of deep interest to every student of history.

3. The Nations and their Governing Signs.

There are many other angles from which we could approach this subject of what predisposes people, nations and races to certain lines of action, making them anti-social or cooperative, and determining their relations with each other. The trend of events at any particular time may not truly reflect these deeper destinies.

It might be of interest here if we continued our study by a consideration of some of the countries and their governing signs. This would be a practical though necessarily a most debatable point. It is not related in any way to the geographical position of these countries but to the destiny (future) and karma (past) of humanity itself as it differentiates itself into nationalities, living at one period of time upon certain territories and so constituting that amalgamation of forms which we call nations or races. Basically and fundamentally the souls, informing these nations or races, remain detached from identification with them until such time as such souls can function on earth. Until, therefore, astrologers know more about group astrology and know also how to determine past influences as well as forecasts, it will not be possible for them to assign the correct ruling signs to the various countries and nations or to check the accuracy or the inaccuracy of the statements which I may make in the following tabulations. That type of astrology which concerns itself with the past, we call *essential astrology* esoterically, in contradistinction to *predictive astrology*. Past conditioning factors are basic and essential to the expression of the present and to what happens in the human family at any given moment, and from a proper understanding of the rules which should (but as yet do not) govern the processes of what is sometimes called the rectifying of a horoscope when the exact moment of birth is not known will come the future science of ascertaining those past facts which produce present occurrences.

You will note that I would differentiate most carefully between countries and nations, owing to the fact that today and increasingly in the future, they will not be synonymous. The British nation is, for instance, a great synthesis of people, as is the United States of America, and also, in a lesser extent, both Brazil and the Argentine. Under the present situation, incident to the war and starting around the year 1900, there is a constant and ceaseless migration of peoples from one place to another and from one country to another, taking place today not only individually but also in group formation. This tends to produce an inevitable fusion, blending and producing inter-racial life, thus constantly offsetting and negating what has been called "racial purity." This attempt at an impossible racial segregation and purity is a misnomer, for the past renders it impossible; mixed blood runs in all veins, but the effort to produce this is the keynote of certain of the more modern cultures. These fortunately are in a minority, for they are anti-evolutionary and their objective is quite impossible of achievement, for they do not start with any pure strain. This tendency towards racial segregation (so noticeable in the Jew and the German) is a form of isolationism and necessarily an aspect of materialism, and is related to the personality of humanity and not to the soul aspect; it is separative in effect and normally feeds pride in the individual and the nation; it runs counter to the true progress of humanity which must lead increasingly to closer human relations, to human wholeness in the truest sense of the term; it will produce the inevitable recognition of vital human unity, placing no emphasis upon individual nations and races. This isolationist spirit was one of the dangers to which the neutral powers were at one time prone, particularly the United States, and the physical warning as to this danger was given to them in the magnetic storms which severed contact between them and Europe and dislocated their relationship between states within America itself.

The world is one world and its sufferings are one; humanity is in truth a unity, but many are still unaware of this and the whole trend of the present teaching is directed to the awakening of humanity to this while there is yet time to avert still more serious conditions. The sins of humanity are also one. Its goal is one and it is as one great human family that we must emerge into the future. I would emphasise this thought: *it is as one humanity, chastened, disciplined but illumined and fused, that we must emerge into the future.* Those who do not grasp this important fact, whether they are what is called belligerents or neutrals, will suffer deeply as a result of their non-participation in the fate of the whole. The isolationist or the super-racial attitudes of the bewildered German people are the attitudes of the separative tendencies of the form nature with its wrong emphasis; but so also is the attitude, veiled under beautiful words and misty idealism, of any neutral power who stands aloof from the happenings of the present. *The Hierarchy is not neutral.* It is one with the right element in every nation and set against all separative, isolationist and materialistic attitudes. Such attitudes prevent the apprehension of the true spiritual values and hinder human development. Identification with all and participation in world conditions—voluntarily and not from force—is the way out today for all peoples. Ponder on this.

1. *The Nations and their Ruling Signs.*

It is, however, obvious that nations react like human beings under the influence of their rays—personality and soul rays—and this is a fact of vital import to the esotericist and something as yet little known or intelligently realised. What I give you, therefore, under this point is new exoterically; attention will have to be paid to the information —either as it comes from me or from other sources—if there is to be real understanding of the situation and therefore useful cooperation with the Forces of Light.

I will give you here the *present* personality influences of the nations, indicated by their governing signs of the zodiac, trusting that you will give due thought to what I impart and assuring you that they are of vital significance at this time, particularly if you compare them with what I gave you anent the rays of the nations in the first volume of *A Treatise on the Seven Rays.* I would remind you that—over the lapse of centuries—nations are reborn several times or come into incarnation in a new form which we may call a period, if unimportant, or a civilsation if significant and dramatic enough. Therefore, the personality ray and the governing influences change with frequency. This is oft forgotten, because the cycles are so much vaster than those of human incarnation. I would also point out that the tabulations which follow agree in part with the ordinary accepted assignment of zodiacal signs to the various countries, but not always. I will give you two signs for each country. One will be the emerging influence which will govern the ego or the soul of the country or nation, and the other that which governs at the present moment the personality ray of the individual country, and so conditions the masses. Forget not that the soul of the people is represented by those who

Country	Ruling Sign	Egoic Ray	Ruling Sign	Personality Ray
Argentina	Cancer ... 4th	Not given	Libra ... 7th	Not given.
Austria	Libra ... 7th	Fourth	Capricorn ... 10th	Fifth.
Belgium	Sagittarius ... 9th	Not given	Gemini ... 3rd	Not given.
Brazil	Leo ... 5th	Fourth	Virgo ... 6th	Second.
China	Taurus ... 2nd	First	Libra ... 7th	Third.
Finland	Capricorn ... 10th	Not given	Aries ... 1st	Not given.
France	Pisces ... 12th	Fifth	Leo ... 5th	Third.
Germany	Aries ... 1st	Fourth	Pisces ... 12th	First.
Great Britain	Gemini ... 3rd	Second	Taurus ... 2nd	First.
Greece	Virgo ... 6th	Not given	Capricorn ... 10th	Not given.
Holland	Aquarius ... 11th	Not given	Cancer ... 4th	Not given.
India	Aries ... 1st	First	Capricorn ... 10th	Fourth.
Ireland	Virgo ... 6th	Not given	Pisces ... 12th	Not given.
Italy	Leo ... 5th	Sixth	Sagittarius ... 9th	Fourth.
Japan	Scorpio ... 8th	Not given	Capricorn ... 10th	Not given.
Poland	Taurus ... 2nd	Not given	Gemini ... 3rd	Not given.
Roumania	Leo ... 5th	Not given	Aries ... 1st	Not given.
Russia	Aquarius ... 11th	Seventh	Leo ... 5th	Sixth.
Scandinavia (4 Nations)	Libra ... 7th	Not given	Cancer ... 4th	Not given.
Spain	Sagittarius ... 9th	Sixth	Capricorn ... 10th	Seventh.
Switzerland	Aries ... 1st	Not given	Aquarius ... 11th	Not given.
Turkey	Cancer ... 4th	Not given	Scorpio ... 8th	Not given.
U. S. A.	Aquarius ... 11th	Second	Gemini ... 3rd	Sixth.

react to the influence of the soul ray and of the sign which is affecting it (its ascendant, one might say), whilst the masses are conditioned by the personality ray and therefore by the sun sign of the specified nation.

NOTE: This tabulation is arranged alphabetically and not in the rate of importance and influence of a country and nation.

It would, I feel, also be of value if I indicated the ruling sign of some of the capital cities of the countries dealt with in the above table. The focus of the immediate response of the peoples of the nations is frequently to be distinguished in *the quality* (if I may so call it) of their capital city and by the decisions there made. I would like to point out that in the British Empire there are several major and distinctive sections which are themselves definitely governed by certain ruling signs; therefore, before giving the rulers of the capitals, I would like to indicate the influences which control the British Empire through the medium of its component parts; they are an important factor in present events, owing to the major and powerful nature of the part Great Britain is playing in the present situation. As you will have noted, Great Britain is ruled by Gemini and Taurus, and consequently the principles of multiplicity and integration are simultaneously present. Duality, triplicity (England, Scotland and Wales) and also differentiation are the conditioning aspects of the empire. Under the major control of Gemini and Taurus you have the following potencies active:

	Egoic Ruler		*Personality Ruler*	
Australia	Virgo	6th	Capricorn	10th.
Canada	Taurus	2nd	Libra	7th
India	Aries	1st	Capricorn	10th
New Zealand	Gemini	3rd	Virgo	6th
South Africa	Aries	1st	Sagittarius	9th.

These are the major divisions. There are lesser divisions but with these I am not here concerned. These countries are related to the mother-country through their planetary rulers, and in this statement you have a definite hint conveyed. The zodiacal signs relate, but the planets are more influential at this stage of evolution.

It is not my intention to give you the ruling signs of the capitals of all the countries; I have dealt with but only the more important:

Country	Capital	Soul Ruler		Personality Ruler	
Belgium	Brussels	Gemini	....3rd	Capricorn	..10th
France	Paris	Virgo	......6th	Capricorn	..10th
Germany	Berlin	Scorpio	....8th	Leo	.........5th
Great Britain	London	Leo	........5th	Libra	.......7th
Italy	Rome	Taurus	....2nd	Leo	.........5th
Poland	Warsaw	Capricorn	.10th	Pisces	......12th
Russia	Moscow	Taurus	....2nd	Aquarius	...11th
United States	Washington	Cancer	.....4th	Sagittarius	..9th

An analysis of the signs ruling the different countries will make certain outstanding conditions apparent and even with the small knowledge of esoteric astrology now available will make certain definite information emerge in your minds as vitally explanatory. Capricorn, for instance, seldom appears as a sign governing the egoic expression of any nation but quite often as governing the personality manifestation, or the exoteric country. Austria, Greece, India, Japan and Spain have Capricorn as their personality rulers, indicating age, crystallisation and materialism; a little study of conditions and the present point in evolution will make this apparent. In the next great and succeeding race to this, Capricorn will appear as ruling the egoic expression, for the soul will then be in greater control and certain great groups of human beings (those who now compose the present nations) will be ready for initiation upon the mountain top of Capricorn.

I cannot spend much time analysing this but would like to indicate one or two points which would serve to guide your thoughts and to clarify the issue. In this manner I can point the way for the future guidance of astrologers who have an esoteric bias. The subject is, however, sufficiently abstruse to deter most people. The relations to be established cannot be based upon some definite starting point, as is sometimes possible in casting the individual horoscope, but upon energy effects, coming direct from the signs themselves, or via certain planetary rulers (again either exoteric, esoteric or hierarchical); these effects are again conditioned by the interplay between the energy of the rays which govern the soul or the personality of the nation or country under consideration. The problem is likewise complicated because there will be the need to distinguish between the horoscope of the territory, housing the nation, and the people themselves who compose that unit which we call a nation. Some nations are fluid and not properly integrated as are the masses of people everywhere; others are integrated entities, or fully expressing personalities; others are crystallised and have nearly run their course as personalities; others again are coming under the influence of their soul ray, leading to another cycle of fluidity, before the definiteness of the initiate-entity becomes apparent; a few again are purely embryonic. Thus the extreme difficulty of the science becomes increasingly apparent. There is, however, no need for discouragement, for this is a science, subject to moments of intense illumination when the intuition will suddenly reveal determining laws and when the capacity to think abstractly and synthetically will pour floods of light upon the most difficult and complex of problems. When the world again settles down to a cycle of peace and with opportunity for further conscious unfoldment, it will be found that that embryonic factor which we call the intuition will flower forth into as recognisable an expression of human consciousness as the present intellectual grasp and mental perception of the race. Until this time comes, the searching astrologer must proceed hopefully but cannot yet expect full understanding of what I here impart.

4. *An Analysis of Certain Countries.*

The horoscope of a country can, therefore, be either that of the soul of the nation or of the personality of the nation, based on the form aspect; there are no means, as yet, of determining the date, for instance, of the birth of a nation or of a race. Boundaries are not determining factors nor is history itself, as now given, an adequate guide. As said above, some nations are entities and demonstrably so, as, for instance, France or Japan; others have been great and powerful nations but are so no longer, but the strain is there, and of these, India and the Jewish race are illustrations. Other nations are, relatively speaking, very modern, as for instance the German nation, yet the strain is very ancient. Strains, types, races, nations, branches and sub-branches produce a bewildering kaleidoscope before which astrology necessarily stands confused. But to the eye of the enlightened esotericist, certain entities emerge clearly and form the nations of the world; the important factor always to remember is that it is *humanity as a whole* which is the factor to be considered. The simile of the human body with its definitely recognised areas of expression, and the organisms which, in their turn, control and condition these areas will be helpful here. The important and the non-important appear; the developing and the vestigial also emerge and under the Law of Correspondences aid in elucidating. In the great body of humanity there are certain areas which vibrate in unison and which attract to themselves souls of a certain quality and keynote; there is a magnetic interplay between countries (territories) and the nations which occupy them. This is not an arbitrary matter but due to magnetic interplay. It is also vibratory interplay, under the great Law of Attraction and Repulsion which has much to do with the intercourse and relationships between nations. Let us now look at a few of them.

France is a Pisces-Leo country, and is expressive egoically of the fifth Ray of Concrete Knowledge or Science and the personality Ray of Active Intelligence. The soul of France, subjectively ruled Europe for the most important and influential part of the Piscean Age, now passing out; she coloured and dominated, by her Leo personality, a large part of the happenings in Europe during the Middle Ages and for centuries; she mediated the Piscean quality to the civilisation of the then known world and her definitely Leo personality—self-conscious, self-centred, brilliantly intelligent and individual—conditioned Europe. It is this Leo personality which is responsible for the intensely nationalistic spirit of the modern French and which negates in them the more Aquarian tendency to universal consciousness or to the expression of the advanced Piscean soul to save the world; *France* comes before the world. The lesson France has to learn today is that the salvation of others is the goal of her Piscean soul and in this the self-interest of Leo precipitates conflict—one to which France is slowly awakening.

The egoic ray of France is that of Concrete Science and this, working in conjunction with the energy of the fifth zodiacal sign, Leo, has given the French people their intellectual brilliance and their scientific bias. The forces of crystallisation pour through Paris which is ruled by Capricorn in its personality and yet the soul of the French nation is nurtured in that great capital through the soul of the city, energised by Virgo and, forget not, that Virgo is the polar opposite of Pisces and the infant Christ in Virgo comes to full flower in Pisces. Here lies the hope of France. You will remember perhaps that some years ago I indicated that from France will come a great psychological or soul revelation which will bring illumination to world thought. If the true Piscean element can be drawn forth and the selfishness and the self-protective interests of the French nation can be offset, France then stands free some day to lead the world spiritually as she has effectively in past history from the more political and cultural aspects, but this can only happen when the personality ray is subordinated to the soul ray and Leo can respond to the Aquarian influence in the coming new era when Aquarius is dominant. The Sun, as the ruler of Leo, made France what she was, irradiating Europe for centuries; but it was the personality and not the spiritual aspect, and her influence at no time was spiritual, as that word should be understood. Esoterically, Pluto, one of the rulers of Pisces, must work, bringing in the death of the personality influence, fostered by Leo; this can be done without any great outer dissolution of the form of the nation through the beneficent influence of Jupiter, the exoteric ruler of Pisces. What is needed in the national life of France is the more spiritual expression of the second Ray of Love-Wisdom, which has in the past led to material success but which can flood the world, via France, once she dies to self. Capricorn, ruling Paris, signifies both death and initiation into the spiritual life, and here lies the choice for France. With the cooperation which Pluto can give in bringing about those conditions which will lead to the revelation of Virgo (ruling the soul of Paris) there is possible— in connection with this powerful and influential country—a contribution to the life of humanity which will be effective in bringing about the new desired conditions in Europe, but France's demand for her personal security must give place to the security of the *whole* from aggression and evil and fear, and all thought of revenge upon or the dismemberment of other countries in the interests of France will have to end, if the true soul of France is to find expression.

Therefore, the following signs (cosmic energy) and planets transmitting solar and cosmic energies, are the conditioning factors of France in incarnation at the present time:

FRANCE

1. Pisces—with its rulers: Jupiter and Pluto. ⎫
2. Leo—with its ruler: the Sun. ⎭ the nation.

3. Virgo—with its rulers: Mercury, Moon, Jupiter. ⎫
4. Capricorn—with its rulers: Saturn and Venus. ⎭ Paris.

5. Ray influences of an indirect nature, coming via the planetary rulers:

   a. Ray 2.—Love-Wisdom, via Jupiter and the Sun. These are the most powerful.

   b. Ray 1.—Power or Will, via Pluto. This is also the Destroyer Ray and can bring the death of the Leo influence.

   c. Ray 3.—Active Intelligence, via Saturn. This co-operates with the third ray personality of France, and at this time Saturn offers most definite opportunity through the focus of power now to be found in Paris.

   d. Ray 4.—Harmony through Conflict, via Mercury. Can France work for world harmony in the post-war period?

   e. **Ray 5.**—Concrete Science or knowledge, via

Venus. In this a realised cooperation with the soul ray, which is also the fifth ray, can bring about, through the French nation, a consummation of the Piscean influence or genius.

f. Ray 4.—This time through the Moon, thus aiding the work of Mercury and producing that needed internal conflict which will release France from Leo and from the control of her self-centred personality.

I would here call your attention to the fact that the astrology which I am emphasising is that which is concerned with the effective energies—what they are and from whence they come. I would repeat here as I have often done before that I am not concerned with predictive astrology. The coming emphasis in astrology will be upon the available energies and the use the subject makes of them and the opportunity which they present at any given time.

I have given you France somewhat in detail so that you can appreciate the extent of the influences which determine any nation and make it for the time what it *is*. The combination of Piscean power in the Piscean Age, plus a potent Leo nature, enabled France at one time to express quite phenomenally its innate subjective tendency to save the world (for France is essentially on the Path of a world Saviour); this was aided by the brilliant clear vision of the fifth and third rays with their intellectual bias, plus the opportunity offered by Saturn, ruling Paris. This enabled France to stage the great French Revolution and strike one of the major blows for the release of humanity from bondage. This has twice occurred during the Piscean Age: once at the signing of the Magna Charta at Runnymede and again at the French Revolution. The recognition of the importance of the rights of humanity, *as a whole,* came to the world via France. It marked a climax and high point in the evolution of the nation. Since then Capricorn and Pluto have produced crystallisation and the death or obscuration temporarily of the then emerging soul aspect (speaking symbolically) and the note of France has not been a selfless one. The forces of the soul are working, but France is as yet predominantly governed by personality and by the selfish aspects of the Leo influences. France, as yet, matters to herself more than humanity matters and the question is: Can she achieve the terrific task of decentralising herself, of sacrificing herself for the common good and of relinquishing her dreams for France in the vision of the whole and so tread again more fully the Path of a World Saviour? There are as yet no signs of this; when the time to make peace treaties arrives, it will become clearer which way France will go and whether she will work for the peace and security of the whole in love and with wisdom, or for France with intellectual brilliance and selfishness.

Let us briefly look at one or two other countries, so enabling students to make comparisons and understand relationships and future possibilities.

Germany is ruled by Aries, bringing in the powerful influences of this first sign in combination with its fourth ray soul (the Ray of Harmony through Conflict). The simple interpretation of this is that we are watching the beginning of a new phase and cycle in the history of the country which emerges into prominence through conflict but which is essentially a process of releasing the soul to fuller expression. It is ruled also by Pisces, cooperating with the influences of its first ray personality, which is the Ray of Power and the Ray of the Destroyer. The whole problem of French-German relations is tied up in this fact for the Piscean soul of

France and the Piscean personality of Germany must eventually come to terms and it is obvious, is it not, that the real solution lies in the hands of France, which must let its soul control? It is because of this that, at the close of the Piscean Age, this whole relationship has come to a focus. France has an integrated personality whilst Germany has *not*; France is mental whilst Germany is predominantly astral; France is, therefore, essentially more potent, and its Leo personality can control with force to the detriment of future world understanding, or its soul can control to the furthering of the ends of the Hierarchy. As you know, Berlin is controlled by Leo from the personality angle, and there again comes out the relationship between the two countries. They are both powerfully influenced by this sign of self-interest and of individuality as well as by Pisces. They cannot escape this relation. Hence the constant clash of these two countries through the dominating self-interest of Leo (ruling both personalities). Engrossment with present attitudes should not lead to forgetfulness of the past. France should not forget the Napoleonic wars, nor Great Britain the Boer war. All nations have much in the past which is apt to be forgotten, particularly if the lessons of greater spiritual growth have been learnt. The United States must not forget either that she is a section of the entire European continent transplanted across the ocean and that European history, successes, mistakes and sins are here also—a thing that many people are very apt to do, thus shifting responsibility. What is happening in the world today is a world happening, not a continental and local occurrence.

Germany is therefore controlled by the following energies and forces, and a study of the consequent inter-relations should prove interesting to the detached and open-minded student.

GERMANY

1. Aries—with its rulers, Mars, Mercury
      and Uranus. ⎫
                   ⎬ the nation.
2. Pisces—with its rulers, Jupiter and Pluto. ⎭
3. Scorpio—with its rulers, Mars and Pluto. ⎫
                                             ⎬ Berlin.
4. Leo—with its ruler, The Sun. ⎭
5. The soul ray. Harmony through Conflict. 4th.
6. Personality ray. Will or Power. 1st.
7. Ray influences of an indirect nature, coming via the planetary rulers:

> **a.** Ray 6.—Idealism or Devotion, via Mars which rules Aries and is the double ruler of Scorpio. This produces the fanaticism and unreasoning devotion and blind acceptance of conditions, so distinctive of the country at this time. It is virtue misdirected.
>
> **b.** Ray 4.—Harmony through Conflict, via Mercury, thus cooperating with the soul ray intensifying the conflicting conditions and leading to a pull between idealism and facts, between France and Germany, and between the groups within Germany itself.
>
> **c.** Ray 7.—Ceremonial Order or Ritual, via Uranus. This affects the masses as a whole, as it is the hierarchical ruler and (because of their point of evolution) leads to their facile standardising and regimenting. The 7th ray also focusses or "grounds the first ray" and leads to the power direction which is given them.
>
> **d.** Ray 2.—Love-wisdom, via Jupiter and the Sun as the ruler of Leo. Thus the personality ray of

the nation and the personality ray of Berlin tend at this stage to express self-love.

e. Ray 1.—Will or Power, via Pluto as the ruler of Pisces, governing the personality of the nation in cooperation with the death giving power of Scorpio which it rules and which governs Berlin. This tremendous activity of the destroying agent as far as Germany is concerned is offset by the influence of Jupiter. It is not nevertheless very potent.

Everything tends to show that the German people, not being an integrated race, are very largely victims and should be just as easily guided into right ways as they have been, at present, guided into their present activities. They did, however, provide a good medium through which the ancient Atlantean conflict could be precipitated and brought to the surface, and the ancient feud between materialism and the Forces of Light be finally resolved for this particular world cycle. Germany is mediumistic, as was its dictator, as I have earlier indicated; it is the Aries-Leo influences which produced the dictator. The Piscean personality of Germany (which is the sign governing mediumship) accounts for the apparently fluid grasp of essentials and the inability of its people and ruling government to stand by pledges. The influence of the sixth ray, coming via Mars, *martially* applied, and the lack of true spiritual love as it is diverted into sentimental personality devotions, account temporarily for the mass negligence to assert itself on behalf of the oppressed and in the interests of the higher principles. The need for this assertion is realised by many in Germany but the negative Piscean personality attitude provides a great obstacle and accounts for what has puzzled all who know and love the German people. At present, the influence of Mars, of Leo and of Pisces in their lower octave or connotations, are dominant. That which can offset this unhappy situation is the influence of Scorpio, the sign of discipleship and one of the death signs in the zodiac.

The struggle for the soul of the people and its emergence into control is really taking place today in Berlin and upon the decision of this conflict much depends. France whose soul is governed by Pisces, the world Saviour, can do much to release the Piscean personality of Germany. Here lies the crux of the world problem. Great Britain, with her soul ray ruled by Gemini (which understands both the soul nature and the personality nature), can do much to help.

I cannot elaborate this further beyond pointing out that both for nations and individuals the first great crisis in Scorpio upon the path of discipleship is determining in its effect upon the future.

In considering Great Britain, we note first that the ruling sign is Gemini from the standpoint of the soul of the people, and that Taurus governs the material outer form of the nation; it is this factor that has led her people to appear before the world under the symbol of John Bull, expressive of the British personality. It has been thought by certain astrologers that Great Britain is ruled by Aries, and this is true of it, as far as that small part which is called England is concerned; but I am dealing with the empire as a whole and not with a fraction of it. It is the Gemini influence that has led to the constant movement and restlessness of the British people; which has led them to cross and recross the ocean and to stage a constant going out to the very ends of the earth, to return ever again to the centre from which they came. This is characteristic of the race. It is the Gemini influence which has produced—viewing the work of the nation from the personality or lower angle— the secret and oft devious diplomacy and subtlety which has in the past distinguished Great Britain's political activity. Gemini people are often distrusted, and the Gemini effect along this line makes of Great Britain no exception. Such distrust has been warranted in the past but is not as justifiable now, for the nation is old and experienced and is fast learning the lessons which she has had to master. As yet, from the higher angle, Gemini does not entirely control, for the soul of Britain is only now struggling for expression. For long ages Taurus has led the way with his material aims, his acquisitive desires, his arrogant will and his blind moving forward towards the possession of that which has been desired. Pervasiveness and movement are two qualities with which Gemini and Taurus have dowered the race. London, the heart centre of the empire is ruled spiritually by Leo and materially by Libra and it is, therefore, the soul factor which links Great Britain to France and which should assist spiritually the Leo nature of the French personality. It is not, however, the spiritual quality of this sign which dominates British policy, but primarily the Libra aspect. Great Britain regards herself as the preserver of the balance of power among the nations and as the one to mete out justice and indicate the right methods of law and order; yet her Gemini nature at times offsets this, whilst Taurus frequently blinds her to the real issues. It is the Leo aspect also which links London to Berlin, but it is Leo in its more self-assertive aspect and hence some of the difficulty and hence also the close and not to be evaded relationship between London-Paris-Berlin, a triangle of force which conditions Europe most potently. It is between these three that the destiny of the race of men in the immediate future lies, and again the question arises: Will the coming decisions be based upon the good of the whole or upon the good of a part of the whole?

It was the Leo force in Great Britain which attracted originally the Leo force in France and led to the Norman conquest in the 11th century. I mention this because it indicates relationship and the demonstrated results of such relations, but not because that past event has any true repercussions at this time.

There is a much closer relation between the United States of America and Great Britain than between any continental power, for Gemini is the ruling sign of both countries, and they have, in many ways, a synchronous vibration. There is however little of the Taurian influence in the States and consequently you have the attitude of frequent misunderstanding which exists between the two powers. They are very close to each other and the welfare of each means much to each of them, so much so that the tendency to misinterpretation of each other's actions and motives is not aided by the fluidity of Gemini. Nevertheless, the arrogance and selfwill of the Bull must give way to the fluid understanding of the inclusive Gemini consciousness, and this is a hard thing for the British temperament at this time to grasp. They are so sure of their rectitude and so convinced of their wisdom that they are apt to forget that good intentions are oft offset by bad methods. The British are just and wise, but their self-sufficient technique and their blindness to other peoples' point of view has not aided world peace and is indicative of the control of Taurus. I would add here that the belief of the German race that they constitute the super-race, the intense nationalism of the French which leads them to feel that they have a superior culture to any other race, the sure pride of the British which leads them to regard themselves as eternally in the right, and the noisy self-assertion of the United States which leads them to regard their country as the hope of the world have in reality little to choose between them and are all equally indicative of personality control. This is, as you know, a thing to be overcome in all nations and individuals.

Governing Great Britain, therefore, are the following energies, working through the zodiacal signs and the ruling planets:

GREAT BRITAIN

1. Gemini—with its rulers, Mercury, Venus and the Earth. } Nation.
2. Taurus—with its rulers, Venus and Vulcan. } Nation.
3. Leo—with its ruler, the Sun. } Capital.
4. Libra—with its rulers, Venus, Uranus and Saturn. } Capital.
5. The soul ray—Love-wisdom. 2nd.
6. The personality ray—Will or Power. 1st.
7. Ray influences of an indirect nature, coming via the planetary rulers:

    a. Ray 4.—Harmony through conflict, via Mercury, leading to a definite link with Germany (as a study of the earlier tabulation will show). It accounts for the warlike history of Great Britain, but works out at the present time in the harmony of the empire.

    b. Ray 5.—Concrete Knowledge or Science, via Venus. It is interesting to note that it is this ray which links Great Britain so closely with France and appears nowhere among the influences which affect the German nation. Venus rules Taurus and Libra as well as Gemini and hence the well developed lower concrete mind of the British nation. The intuitive mind however needs development.

c. Ray 3.—Active Intelligence or Adaptability, via the Earth and also via the planet Saturn as it appears among the rulers of Libra. Here you have the clue as to why the British Empire covers the Earth, for there is a close connection between the Earth, as a whole, and Great Britain. It links Great Britain also with the third ray personality of France.

d. Ray 1.—Will or Power, via the planet Vulcan. There is in the first ray—as it expresses itself through Vulcan—very little of the Destroyer aspect as there is in the planetary influence of Pluto, another agent of the first ray. Again you find in this ruler of Great Britain's Taurian personality, a link with the first ray German personality. It accounts also for the forging of the chains which tie the Empire together, making it a unity through the will of the people.

e. Ray 2.—Love-wisdom, via the Sun, the ruler of Leo which governs the soul of London, and which is also a channel for the soul force of the British empire which is essentially that of love-wisdom when given real expression and not controlled and dominated by the Libra influence.

f. Ray 7.—Ceremonial Order or Organized Ritual, reaching our planet via Uranus and giving to the empire its grounded physical plane control over place and circumstance, its legal fundamentals, in cooperation with Libra, and its love of order and of rule, thus providing full expression for the first ray energies of the British Empire.

A study of the interplay of these energies and forces will account adequately for Great Britain and her activities; they indicate also certain definite lines of affinity and also point the way to imminent possibilities of adjustment, if the love which is the basic motivating power of the British soul is permitted expression. Hitherto it has been primarily Taurus and Leo as well as Libra which have coloured British attitudes, decisions and activities. Can Britain change and —preserving the will-to-order and the balanced judgment which Libra confers upon her—eliminate the Taurian aspects which have led her blindly to seek that which she desires and because of her powerful personality to gain those ends? There is an ironic fate which determines that this great nation, having in past centuries been one of the major aggressors of the world, should now bring to an end, with the aid of France (which has a very similar aggressive tendency), the period of aggression, and so be used to inaugurate an age of cooperation, of understanding and of mutually shared responsibility. The future of the world lies at present largely in the hands of France and Great Britain, and the happiness of the world is assured if the soul energy of both these countries controls, and personality aims and ambitions are negated.

I can only most briefly touch upon the energies which motivate and condition the Italian empire and the United States, leaving you to make your deductions and applications. Russia is as yet embryonic and her part lies more in the East than in the West, provided she follows the indicated lines. Her two ruling signs are Aquarius and Leo and her real function in the comity of nations lies far ahead when the Aquarian age is flourishing and the Leo control of the Russian personality has been offset. The planets which primarily influence Russia are the Sun (2nd ray), Uranus (7th ray), Jupiter (2nd ray) and the Moon (4th ray). This makes a most interesting, a most humanitarian and—in the long run—a non-destructive combination. At present, the intensely individualistic Leo force in its worst aspects are dominating, but this will not last as history will eventually prove. The noisy, cruel child can turn into a controlled humanitarian in adult life and the influences potent in the Russian horoscope indicate this.

Again, in Italy, you find Leo appearing, thus relating Italy to France, to Great Britain and to Berlin—all of which have Leo as a ruling sign, either of the nations themselves or of their chief city. There is, consequently, no possibility of any of these four powers being able to evade relationships. Italy is more closely related to Great Britain than she is to France, because Rome is ruled by Taurus and by Leo which ties her to Great Britain through identity of vibration. This France will have to recognise as well as Italy and Great Britain.

The personality of Italy is ruled by Sagittarius, the sign of the one-pointed disciple, and it is owing to this that we have the undeviating aim of the Italian state and its refusal to be moved from certain attitudes and determinations. Italy sees more clearly than Germany the principles involved at this time, and though Rome is blinded at times by the Taurian influence which leads to a blind rushing forward towards a goal, irrespective of consequences and implications, yet essentially the inner straight line of foreseen and planned activity will hold Italy true to the objective.

The following conditioning forces make the story of Italy sufficiently clear:

ITALY

1. Leo—with its ruler, the Sun.
2. Sagittarius—with its rulers, Jupiter, the ⎫ Nation.
      Earth and Mars. ⎭

3. Taurus—with its rulers, Venus and Vulcan. ⎫ Capital.
4. Leo—with its ruler, the Sun. ⎭

5. Soul ray—Ideals, Devotion. 6th.
6. Personality. Harmony through conflict. 4th.
7. Ray influences of an indirect nature, coming through the planetary rulers:

   a. Ray 2.—Love-wisdom, via the Sun and Jupiter. This again relates Italy to the second ray soul of Great Britain and tends to a basic understanding. I would here point out that in this second ray influence it is the wisdom aspect more than the love aspect which is dominant. Love is in reality, understanding wisdom in active expression.

   b. Ray 3.—Active Intelligence, via the Earth. It was this Earth influence which, in the past, gave Italy her world dominion and which swayed the Italian personality towards the thought of another worldwide empire.

   c. Ray 6.—Devotion and Idealism, via Mars. I would remind you that the soul ray of Italy is also the sixth ray. You have, therefore, the influence of Mars dominating Italian and Roman history, and it is this martian tendency which lay at the base of the German Italian axis. It, however, is *not* today the controlling factor.

   d. Ray 5.—Concrete Knowledge or Science, via Venus. This influence is also dominant in Great

Britain and again closely relates the two countries. Of this there is one curious little instance, which demonstrates an almost uniform working of this scientific bent for the good of the entire world (Venus in relation with Jupiter). That is the invention of the telephone by Alexander Graham Bell and the development of the radio by Marconi.

e. Ray 1.—Will or Power, via Vulcan, the forger and the worker in metals whose influence in this case closely associates itself with the undeveloped aspect of the Leonian influence.

In the above hints you may find much that is explanatory and much that will clarify British-Italian relations. The destinies of the two countries are closely allied and together they can potently affect the German race and influence it towards a better adjustment to life and a wiser discrimination. It will require the backing of France, when the soul of that country controls.

We will just look at the controlling factors in one other country, the United States of America, and indicate the influences working at this time which are in process of bringing to an end the adolescent stage in that country and enabling it to come forth in full maturity.

This vast land is ruled by Gemini, linking it therefore closely with Great Britain and also by Aquarius as the ruler of its soul ray. This combination of a sixth ray personality, ruled by Gemini, and a second ray soul (as has Great Britain), ruled by Aquarius, is potent for future power and usefulness. The capital city, Washington, is ruled by Cancer and Sagittarius, and it is this fact which leads the United States to act like the Crab (Cancer) and be pre-occupied with its own house which it carries heavily on its back and to vanish into hiding at the first signs of trouble. Because also the Sagittarian influence is strong, there is a potent determination to stick one-pointedly to any decision made. This its sixth ray personality enforces at times almost to the point of a fanatical blindness and to the detriment of the long range vision which is needed at such times as these.

Like Russia, this country is in the making and—as I have told you elsewhere—as the nation's power shifts, as it will and as it now really is shifting from Washington to New York, the Cancerian influence will steadily lessen and the country will take its place as an adult among the nations. Its Gemini nature and its Aquarian soul should (when developed and balanced) provide a most remarkable channel for human expression. You will note that none of its zodiacal rulers link it with France, except indirectly through Cancer, which is the polar opposite of Capricorn, one of the rulers of Paris. It is for this reason that such a small percentage, relatively speaking, of French people migrate to the States; there is a closer link with Italy than with France, and hence the large Italian population, for Sagittarius rules both Italy and Washington. The influences are, therefore, as follows:

1. Aquarius—with its rulers, Uranus, Jupiter and the Moon.
2. Gemini—with its rulers, Mercury, Venus and the Earth.

} Nation.

3. Cancer—with its rulers, the Moon and Neptune.
4. Sagittarius—with its rulers, Jupiter, the Earth and Mars.

} Capital.

5. The soul ray—Love-wisdom, 2nd.
6. Personality ray—Idealism Devotion. 6th.

7. Indirect influences via the planetary rulers are many, and the rays conditioning this country are consequently many, owing to the mixture of races found there. Of these influences there are eleven in all, for the Earth presents two aspects and the Moon veils both Vulcan and Uranus.

   a. Ray 7.—Order and Magic, via Uranus. This influence is inherited from the Atlantean world, which still rules the territorial aspect of the States, which is a remnant of old Atlantis. It is this that produces the many magical, spiritualistic and occult groups which flourish today in the States.

   b. Ray 2.—Love-wisdom, via Jupiter, thus linking the States closely with Great Britain and indirectly with France.

   c. Ray 4.—Harmony through Conflict, via the Moon veiling in this case the planet Vulcan. Vulcan here "forges on his anvil, through fire and blows, that linking network which covers all the nation and makes it hold together." This ray produces the condition which brings together Germany and the States, for the fourth ray is the German soul ray and the first ray, which Vulcan transmits via the Moon, links the German soul and personality to the United States. Hence the vast numbers of Germans who come to the States in order to escape from the personality activity of Germany as it expresses itself through its first ray destroyer aspect.

   d. Ray 4.—I enumerate this ray for the second time because it expresses itself here through Mercury the Messenger, and emphasises *the harmony aspect* in contradistinction to the conflict angle which the Moon and Vulcan together have precipitated. It is the Moon-Vulcan relation which produces the political conflict which always rages in the States.

e. Ray 5.—Concrete Knowledge and Science, via Venus. This confers the intelligence which is so marked in the American people and will eventually determine the lines along which their education will run and their religious organisations.

f. Ray 3.—Active Intelligence or Adaptability, via the Earth, thus 'grounding' the American people and basically making the soil their problem. Hence the prominence of agriculture in the public consciousness and the pre-occupation of the government with cotton problems, the corn belt problem and many other issues of moment.

g. Ray 6.—Idealism or Devotion, via Mars. This greatly augments the power of the sixth ray personality of the States, thus presenting very real problems in a young people who are apt always to be fanatical and exclusive. Exclusiveness is one of the major weaknesses of the sixth ray type.

h. Ray 4.—This influence appears, as you see, frequently, but this time it is through the Moon as it veils Uranus. This produces a conflict of a different nature than that which takes place when the Moon veils Vulcan or transmits the energy of the fourth ray direct. Uranus is the medium for the 7th ray and the function of its blending with the fourth, via the Moon, is to bring about a magical relationship between the many diverse nationalities found in the States and so fuse and blend them into an homogeneous whole—which is not the case at this time.

Thus the influences pouring into the United States today are very many; they relate the country practically to every country in Europe; this leads at times to chaotic conditions and to much confusion of thought. Yet it produces a rich-ness in the national life which is a good augury for the future. A study of what I have said and a consideration of the various tabulations will prove how utterly impossible it is for the American people to dissociate themselves from Europe and the rest of the world.

5. *The Significance of Certain Cities.*

These energies which we have been considering are released into our planetary life through the medium of certain great inlets. At this time there are five such inlets, scattered over the world. Wherever one of these inlets for spiritual force is found, there will also be present a city of spiritual importance in the same location. These five points of spiritual influx are:

1. London. . . . For the British Empire.
2. New York. .For the Western Hemisphere.
3. Geneva. . . . .For Europe, including the U.S.S.R.
4. Tokyo. . . . . For the Far East.
5. Darjeeling. .For India and the greater part of Asia.

Later, two more points for energy will be added to these but the time is not yet. Through these five places and the areas in their neighborhood the energy of five rays pours forth, conditioning the world of men, leading to results of profound significance and determining the trend of events. These five points of conditioning energy (in spite of the fact that the energy pouring through Darjeeling has not yet reached its full strength) produce two triangles of force in their inter-relations:

1. London. New York. Darjeeling.
2. Tokyo. New York. Geneva.

Geneva and Darjeeling are two centres through which pure spiritual energy can be directed with more facility than through the other three; they, therefore, constitute the higher points of their respective triangles. They are also more subjective in their influence than are London, New York or Tokyo Together they form the five centres of "impelling energy" today.

It may interest you also to know the governing rays and the astrological signs of these five centres, but it must not be forgotten that the personality rays change from period to period in connection with countries and cities just as with individual human beings:

City	Soul	Personality	Sign
London	5th ray	7th ray	Gemini.
New York	2nd ray	3rd ray	Cancer.
Tokyo	6th ray	4th ray	Cancer.
Geneva	1st ray	2nd ray	Leo.
Darjeeling	2nd ray	5th ray	Scorpio.

If students will study this information in connection with that given elsewhere in connection with the nations and other cities, the inter-relations now emerging in world affairs will be seen as the result of the play of these forces and energies and as, therefore, to a certain extent, unavoidable. The use of the energy may be along wrong lines, producing separation and trouble; it may be along right lines, leading to eventual harmony and understanding; but the energy is there and must make its effects felt. As in the individual life, as the results of the play of soul energy upon the form aspect, one or other of the rays will dominate. If the person or the nation is spiritually oriented, the result of the energy impact will be good and will lead towards the working out of the divine plan, and thus be wholly constructive. Where personality force dominates, the effects will be destructive and may temporarily hinder divine Purpose. Nevertheless, even force which is turned to destructive ends can and does finally work towards good, for the trend of the evolutionary force is unalterable, being based on the Will-to-good of Divinity Itself. The inpouring soul energy can be slowed down or speeded on its way according to the purpose, aspiration and the orientation of the entity (human or national); it can express soul purpose or personality selfishness, but the innate urge to betterment will inevitably triumph.

This entire question of the planetary centres and the energy which they release is naturally of great interest and, could we but realise it, of supreme importance. Some great truth lies veiled behind the tendency of all peoples to regard certain cities and places as holy and as set apart for their spiritual value; they make them the goal of their pilgrimages; in connection with the human being, the same analogy holds good and the heart, for some reason, is regarded as holier and more desirable in its expression than the head. All this indicates an innate recognition by humanity that behind the outer form is ever to be found the intangible, the real and the holy.

I would like to enlarge somewhat upon this subject of the centres through which spiritual energy is today flowing, but it must be remembered that the theme with which we are now occupied is one of general interest but not of individual moment. Arguing as one ever should from the universal to the particular, it is essential that humanity relate its own mechanism to the greater mechanism (our entire planetary life) and view what is called "one's own soul" as an infinitesimal part of the world soul. It is necessary also for man to relate his soul to his personality, viewing both as aspects and integral parts of the human family. This will be increasingly the case. This process is beginning to demonstrate in the steadily expanding group, national and racial consciousness which humanity is today demonstrating—a consciousness which shows as a spiritual inclusiveness or as an abnormal and wicked attempt (from the standpoint of the soul) to fuse and blend all nations into a world order, based on material issues and dominated by a material vision. There was nothing spiritual in the vision of the leaders of the powers which were called the Axis powers, and the vision of the masses of people has not proved adequate to arrest, as yet, the materialising of this vision. But the spiritual intent of mankind is slowly growing and the great Law of Contrasts will eventually bring illumination.

The Lord of the World, the "Ancient of Days," is releasing new energies into humanity, transmuted in the present furnace of pain and fiery agony. This transmutation will bring about a new power of sacrifice, of inclusive surrender, a clearer vision of the Whole and a cooperative spirit hitherto unknown and which will be the first expression of that great *principle of sharing,* so sorely needed today.

I am not here speaking idealistically or mystically. I am pointing out an immediate and possible goal; I am giving a clue to a scientific process which is going on under our eyes and which is, at this time, at a point of crisis.

As this is the Aryan race (the term is not used in the German or materialistic sense) these five centres to which reference has been made, these five focal points of spiritual energy, are being abnormally and deliberately stimulated and vitalized. The energy which flows from them is profoundly affecting the world and the United Nations; this holds great hope for the future. It is for the reason that New York is one of these five centres that the United Nations organization is to work here.

There are two centres on our planet which are as yet relatively quiescent as far as any world effect is concerned. To them I assign no other focal point beyond hinting that within the continent of Africa one will some day be found, and later still (many millions of years later) another will be discovered in the region of Australia. It is, however, with the five centres in this fifth rootrace that we are concerned.

The force which the centre at Geneva is expressing (at present ineffectually, though later a change will come) is that of the second Ray of Love-Wisdom, with its major emphasis at this time upon the quality of inclusiveness. It is concerned with the "binding together in brotherly love" and with the expression of the nature of service. This planetary centre, which conditions the little country of Switzerland, has had a most potent effect upon that country and a study of these effects will demonstrate future possibility for the world, once the flow of its energy is less obstructed. It has produced the fusion of three powerful racial types in group formation and not through admixture as in the United States; it has enabled two relatively antagonistic divisions of the Christian faith to work together with a minimum of friction; it has made Geneva the seat of the Red Cross—that world activity which works truly impartially with and for the nationals of all countries and for the prisoners of all nations; it housed that sad though well-intentioned experiment which was called the League of Nations, and will again house a more true league to meet the world need; it is that which protected the small country from the aggressive sweep of the Axis powers. The motto or note of this centre is "I seek to fuse, to blend and serve."

The force which is centered in London is that of the first Ray of Will or Power in its building aspect and not in its destroying aspect. It is the service of the whole which is being attempted and at great cost, and the effort is to express the Law of Synthesis which is the new emphasis pouring through from Shamballa. Hence the fact that the governments of many nations found asylum in Great Britain during the war. Also, *if* the Forces of Light triumph because of the cooperation of mankind, the energy expressing itself through this powerful empire will be potent in establishing a world order of intelligent justice and a fair economic distribution. The keynote of this force is "I serve."

The force expressing itself through the centre, New York, is the force of the sixth Ray of Devotion or Idealism. Hence the conflicts everywhere to be found between the varying ideologies, and the major conflict between those who stand for the great ideal of world unity brought about by a united effort of the Forces of Light, backed by the cooperative effort of all the democratic nations, and the separative materialistic attitude of those who seek to keep the United States from assuming responsibilities and her rightful place in world affairs. This latter group, if they succeed in their endeavour, will deny the United States her share in the "gifts of the Gods in the coming age of peace which will succeed this present point of critical suspension," as *The Old Commentary* phrases it. The sixth Ray is either

militant and active, or mystical, pacific and futile, and these
two aspects at present condition the United States. The
keynote of this world centre is "I light the WAY;" this is
the privilege of the States if its people so choose and permit
worldwide humanitarian, self-sacrifice (self-initiated) and
a firm decision to stand by righteousness to govern their
present attitudes and policies. This is slowly coming to
pass and the selfish voices of the blind idealists, the fearful
and the separative are dying out. All this is happening
under the inspiration of service, motivated by love. Thus
the two major democracies can eventually restore world
order, negate the old order of selfishness and aggression
and usher in the new order of world understanding, world
sharing and world peace. Peace will be the result of understanding and sharing, and not the origin of them, as the
pacifists so often imply.

The force pouring through Darjeeling at this time
is that of the first Ray of Will or Power. The soul ray
of India is the first ray and hence the immediate effect of
the inpouring Shamballa force is to stimulate the will-to-
power of all dictators, whether they are the would-be world
dictators such as Hitler and his group of evil men, ecclesi-
astical dictators in any religion, business dictators in any
business group in any part of the world, or those minor
dictators, the tyrants in the home. It is interesting to note
that the keynote of India is "I hide the light," and this has
been interpreted to mean that the light pours forth from
the East and that the gift of India to the world is the light
of the Ageless Wisdom. This is true in a sense, but there
is a wider and deeper sense in which it will prove true.
When the intent and purpose of the great Life which works
through Shamballa is carried out and is in process of expression, a light will be revealed which has never yet been

seen or known. There is a word in the Christian Scriptures which says "In that light shall we see light;" this means that through the medium of the light of wisdom shed abroad in our hearts through the Ageless Wisdom, we shall eventually see *the Light of Life* itself—something meaningless and inexplicable to humanity at present but which will be later revealed when the present point of crisis is surmounted. Of its nature and its effect I have naught to say to you at present.

I would like here to interpolate some remarks. It is of deep moment to realise that Great Britain and the United States are closely related; that this relation makes certain realities and activities inevitable once the soul of each nation is functioning potently. India and Great Britain are also related through this first Ray personality of Great Britain and the soul ray of India. The implications are clear and interesting and also encouraging. The consciousness aspect of the British people is steadily shifting into an expression of their second ray soul and hence their seizing upon the opportunity at this time to serve humanity at immense cost. The same thing is happening to the American people. The problem of shifting idealism is great, as I have said, and the temptation is to hide behind the glamour of fighting for an ideal rather than react to world need, and omit to react to the ray of the soul which is the second ray of love.

The forces flowing through Tokyo are those of the first Ray in its lower materialistic aspect. Japan is governed by the soul ray in the consciousness of its leaders. Its sixth ray personality is responding to the call of the first ray energy and hence all the present unhappy attitudes and activities, and hence also its link with Germany through the soul ray of both nations and with Italy through the personality rays. Hence, therefore, the Axis.

I would here point out that in these inter-relations is
no inevitable fate or unavoidable destiny. The aim of the
individual disciple is to handle the forces which play
through him in such a manner that only constructive good
can eventuate. He can misuse energy or employ it for soul
ends. So it is with nations and races. The fate of a nation
lies in the hands of its leaders usually; they marshal the
nation's forces, focus the national intent (if intuitive
enough) and develop the characteristics of the people,
leaving in fact behind them the memory of symbols of
national intent, ideals or corruption. This can be seen as
it worked out in a demonstrable way in the two great
guiding groups of world leaders during the war. The three
Axis groups of leaders, dominated by the evil German
group, with Italy and Japan fighting at intervals against the
evil influence (consciously seldom but unconsciously often),
and the second group—the leaders of the Allied Cause. No
matter what past history may indicate in connection with
many of the allied nations (past aggressions, ancient
cruelties and wrong doing), they were and are today seeking to cooperate with the Forces of Light and are endeavouring to salvage human freedom—political, religious
and economic.

I would also point out in passing that the two major
divisions of the world—the Occident and the Orient—are
also governed by certain ray energies, as follows:

The Occident......Soul Ray...........Ray II.
                  Personality Ray......Ray IV.

The Orient........Soul Ray...........Ray IV.
                  Personality Ray......Ray III.

I would remind you that we are in a period of shifting rays and that they change both for individuals and nations, for hemispheres and planets. All can move off a minor ray on to a major, if destiny decrees. A study of the above tabulation will give much light to the inter-human relation. Three great countries hold the destiny of humanity in their hands at this time: The United States of America, Great Britain and Russia. Great fusing, racial experiments are going on in all these lands; the rule of the people is being developed in all of them, though it is as yet in an embryonic stage. In Russia it is being retarded by a dictatorship which will shortly end; in the States by corrupt politics, and in Great Britain by ancient imperialistic tendencies. But democratic principles are being developed, if not controlling; religious unity is being established though it is not yet functioning, and all three countries are learning very rapidly, though the United States at present is learning the most slowly.

The Occident and the Orient are linked through the personality ray of the Occident and the soul ray of the Orient; this indicates eventual understanding, once the second ray occidental soul becomes the dominant factor. When these various relationships are somewhat grasped by the peoples of the world, you will get the clue to the various happenings taking place today and will understand the goal and the method of its attainment more clearly. There is much deep research work to be done, for the science of energy relationships is yet in its infancy.

The next few years will see its gain. What is really happening is a shift in the human consciousness from its focus on individual energies functioning through some specific ring-pass-not (individual, national, continental or racial) to a grasp of their inter-relation and effects upon each other This science can be studied in various ways:

1. From the angle of antagonisms which seem inevitable and which can be accounted for by the ray energies and which can be offset by soul energies rightly employed.
2. From the angle of identity of forces, leading inevitably to identity of interests and activities.
3. From the angle of fusion, of unity of vision and of goals.
4. From the angle of humanity as a whole. If it is remembered that humanity is primarily governed by two rays (the second and the fourth) it will be found that those nations and countries whose governing rays are also the second and the fourth must and will play an important part in determining human destiny.

Therefore, through the five major centres in the planet today, spiritual energy is streaming forth, and according to the vehicle of expression which receives its impact so will be the reaction and activity, and so will be the type of consciousness interpreting and using it. The ancient occult truism remains accurate: "Consciousness is dependent upon its vehicle for expression and both are dependent upon life and energy for existence." This remains an immutable law.

The five cities which are the exoteric expression of the esoteric centre of force and through which the Hierarchy and Shamballa are seeking to work are the correspondence in the planetary body to the four centres up the spine and the ajna centre in the body of humanity and of individual man. In all three cases, they are "living vital focal points of dynamic force" to a greater or less extent. Some predominantly express soul energy and some personality force; some are influenced by Shamballa and some by the Hierarchy. The head centre of the Occident is beginning to react to second ray energy and the ajna centre to fourth ray energy and in this lies the hope of the race of men.

There is a wide field of research here. This research will fall into several categories:

1. Research into the realities of man's spiritual nature and centres, the nature and influences of their governing planets, their inter-relation from the energy angle and the quality of the ray forces which are seeking expression, plus a knowledge of the personality and egoic rays. Out of this will come an understanding grasp of the human constitution which will reveal all relationships and produce two basic "events in time":

   a. The blending in the waking consciousness of the subjective and objective life of the individual.

   b. A new relation established between men which will be based upon the above fusion.

2. Research into the various national centres and their esoteric ruling energies, revealing in a more universal manner and with a wider horizon the destiny of humanity in relation to its group units, large and small. The soul and personality qualities of nations will be studied, the centres within each nation which focus certain ray energies will be noted, and the qualitative emanations of its five or six major cities will be investigated. Let me here give you an instance of what I mean: the influences of New York, Washington, Chicago, Kansas City and Los Angeles will be the subject of scientific research; the psychic atmosphere and the intellectual appeal will be studied, effort will be made to discover the soul quality and the personality nature (the spiritual and the materialistic tendencies) of these great aggregations of human beings which have come into expression in certain fixed localities

because they are expressions of the force centres in the vital body of the nation.

Similarly, in connection with the British Empire, a study will be made of London, Sydney, Johannesburg, Toronto and Vancouver with subsidiary studies of Calcutta, Delhi, Singapore, Jamaica and Madras which are all subjectively related in a manner unforeseen by students at present. Under the plan, and contingent upon the energies pouring through the five planetary centres according to plan, there are three great fusing energies or vital centres present upon our planet:

a. Russia, fusing and blending eastern Europe and western and northern Asia.

b. The United States (and later South America), fusing and blending central and western Europe and the entire western hemisphere.

c. The British Empire, fusing and blending races and men throughout the entire world.

In the hands of these nations lies the destiny of the planet. These are the three major world blocs, from *the consciousness angle* and from the angle of world synthesis. Other and lesser nations will participate in the process with full independence and cooperation, voluntarily and through the perfecting of their na-tional life in the interests of the whole of humanity and through the desire to express and preserve their soul integrity and their purified national purpose (which purification is now going on). The keynote, however, of human living will be struck by Russia, Great Britain and the United States—not because of their power, their historical past and their material resources or territorial extent, but because they are in a position to fuse and blend the many types, because they are far-visioned in their world purpose, because they are not basically selfish in their intent, and because the government of the peoples reaches down into the depths of each nation and is fundamentally *for the people*. Their basic Constitution, Magna Charta and Bill of Rights are human. Other nations will be gradually swept into line with these fundamental spiritual requirements, or —if they are already based on these human principles and not on the rule of a powerful minority, exploiting an unhappy majority—they will cooperate freely with these greater nations in a federation of purposes and of interests until such time as all the nations of the world see the vision clear, forego their selfish aims and agree in the unity of the work to be done for the whole. Humanity will then emerge into the light of freedom with a revealed beauty and a spiritual purpose, hitherto unknown.

Beginning as ever with the study of the microcosm as the clue to the macrocosm, but seeking at the same time to envisage the macrocosm in order to understand the microcosm, man will some day establish an intelligent relation to the whole of which he is a part and with conscious cooperation. Thus the higher mind and the lower mind, the abstract and the concrete, the subjective and the objective will be brought into a functioning unity and man will be *whole*.

I cannot give you the relation of the planetary centres to the human being. Too much knowledge would be given too soon and prior to the time when there is enough love present in human nature to offset the possible misuse of energy with its often disastrous consequences. The colours, the mathematical rate of the higher vibrations which emanate from the centres—individual and planetary—and the quality (esoterically understood) of the energies must be the subject of human research and self-ascertained. The clues and the hints have been given in the Ageless Wisdom. The slower method of research is the safer at present. Early in the next century, an initiate will appear and will carry on this teaching.

The remainder of this century must be dedicated to rebuilding the shrine of man's living, to reconstructing the form of humanity's life, to reconstituting the new civilisation upon the foundations of the old, and to the reorganising of the structures of world thought, world politics, plus the redistribution of the world's resources in conformity to divine purpose. Then and only then will it be possible to carry the revelation further.

Be of good cheer, for there is no true defeat of the human spirit; there is no final extinction of the divine in man, for divinity ever rises triumphant from the darkest pit of hell. There is need, however, to overcome the inertia of the material nature in response to human need, individually and by the nations not engrossed with the essentials of the situation. This shows signs of happening. There is no power on Earth which can prevent the advance of man towards his destined goal and no combination of powers can hold him back. Today that combination is active—a combination of ancient evil and modern aggressive selfishness, released through a group of unscrupulous and ambitious men in every country. They will not finally succeed. They may delay and hinder the emergence of freedom. The charge against them under the Lords of Destiny is mounting up, but Divinity will triumph.

6. *Spiritual life in the New Age.*

One point I would like here to bring to your attention and that is that the two great groups of divine agents—the Great White Brotherhood and the Lodge of Materialistic Forces—are both of them seeking to divert these energies into channels which will further the ends for which they work and for which they were formed and exist. There-fore, I would ask you to remember that behind all the outer events are these two directing agencies. You have, as a consequence:

1. Two groups of advanced Minds, both groups equally illumined by the light of the intellect, and both of them formulating clearly their objectives, but differing in their direction and their emphasis. One group, under the divine plan, works with the form aspect entirely, and in this group the light of love and of selflessness is absent. The other group is working entirely with the soul or the consciousness aspect, and in this group the doctrine of the heart and the law of love control.

   In this connection, the two groups are working in opposition, therefore, upon the mental plane.

2. The plans, which embody these two differing ideals and objectives, are next carried down on to the astral plane, and thus into the world of desire. The lines of demar-cation remain ever entirely clear as far as the workers in these two groups are concerned, but are not so clear where ordinary human beings and the world disciples and initiates are concerned. There is much chaos on the plane of desire, and the world Arjuna is today sitting in bewilderment between the two opposing forces or camps, recognising his relationship both to form and to

soul and at the same time wondering where his duty lies. His point in evolution determines his problem.

Thus the two groups are working in opposition upon the plane of desire.

3. The materialising of the plans of these two groups of illumined minds proceeds steadily under the differing laws of their being—the laws of form life and the laws of spiritual living. In this initial stage and whilst the battle is being fought out in the realm of desire (for that is where the major conflict is being waged, and all that is happening upon the physical plane is only a reflection of an inner conflict) the forces of these two groups, working with the energies of the sixth and seventh rays, have brought about in the field of physical living, a state of complete cataclysm. The economic situation and the religious hatreds are the two major instruments. This is a subject upon which you would do well to ponder.

Consequently, you have two groups, two objectives, two great formulated ideals, two streams of active energy and two rays predominantly in conflict, thus producing the differing ideologies. The result of this dualism is the external chaos, the differentiation of the two group ideals into the many human experiments, and the resultant ranging of the entire human family under many banners, which testify to the various viewpoints in the many fields of thought—political, religious, economic, social, educational and philosophical. The result of all this conflict is, I would tell you, definitely *good,* and it demonstrates the steady achievement of the Great White Lodge. The consciousness of humanity has been definitely expanded and the whole world of men at this time is thinking. This is a totally new phenomenon and a fresh experience in the life of the human soul. The first result of all the turmoil has been to shift the focus of human attention on to the mental plane and thereby nearer to the sources of light and love.

It is right here and in connection with this eventful change of focus that the world disciples can shoulder responsibility and proceed to active work. When I here speak of disciples, I am using the term in connection with all who aspire to true humanity, to brotherhood, and to the living expression of the higher and spiritual values. I am not using it altogether in the technical sense, which involves a recognised relation to the Hierarchy through the grades of probationary or accepted discipleship, though these are included in my thought. I refer to all aspirants and to all who have any sense of true values and an urge to meet the world's need.

To understand a little the problem involved and the differing modes of work which characterise those who worked in the past under the influence of the sixth ray and those who are learning to work under the influence of the incoming seventh ray, it might be helpful if we compared very briefly the two systems of activity. I would ask you to remember that both systems and modes of work are equally right in their time and place, but that the modern disciple should be discarding the old methods and steadily learning to employ the new and more modern and effective modes of work. This he must learn to do optimistically and with assurance, knowing that the benefits and the experience gained under the sixth ray system of discipline is still his most precious possession because it has been transmuted from method and mode into characteristics and established habits. It is the new ways of working and the new forces and objectives which the disciple of this present era has to master; he must do this relying upon the lessons learnt in the past and must base his new structure of truth upon the foundations and the stabilised orientations, which must now be established.

The first step for the sincere aspirant is at this point to stop for a moment to enquire and discover whether he is working primarily under the sixth ray impulse or the seventh ray influence. I use these words "impulse and influence" deliberately because they describe the general effect of the two functioning energies. Upon one thing all disciples and aspirants can rely and this is the basic and enduring effect of all the sixth ray potencies which have been established during the past two thousand years. These must be counted upon, offset and understood and the newer influence must then be studied, the newer methods investigated and mastered, and the new ideas and idealisms must be brought through into objectivity and so expressed in a new way. Only thus can the new civilisation and culture be wisely and sanely produced and the foundations laid for the development of the human family along right lines during the coming era. It will be of value, therefore, to compare the old and the new ways of discipline and of training, of attribute and quality, and of method and objectives.

Let us take the sixth ray methods of activity and its major characteristics first of all. They are, for us, the most familiar and can be rapidly considered, enabling us to pass on to the new ways of demonstrating and discovering the ancient wisdom, and to the comprehension of the fresh modes of working which will give new vitality to the work of the Hierarchy upon the physical plane.

The outstanding characteristic of the disciple and the aspirant under the old regime was *devotion*. The race had of necessity, to achieve a different and right orientation to the world of spiritual values, and hence the effort of the Hierarchy during the past twenty centuries was to lay the emphasis upon the realm of religious values. The world religions have held the centre of the stage for several thousand years in an effort to make humanity seek one-pointedly for the soul and thus prepare itself for the emergence of the fifth kingdom in nature. This is slated (if I might use such a specialised word) to come into manifestation during the imminent Aquarian age; this age will be predominantly the age of worldwide discipleship, leading later to the age of universal initiation in Capricornian times. Therefore the great world religions have held authoritative sway for a very long time; their peculiar tenets, adapted to specific nation, race or time, embodied some truth through the medium of some particular teacher who attracted to himself individuals throughout the world who were spiritually minded, because he expressed for them the highest goal towards which they could possibly strive. All the world religions have been thus built around an embodied Idea, Who, in His Own Person, expressed the immediate ideal of the time and age. He demonstrated certain divine attributes and concepts which it was necessary to present to the vision of the sons of men as their possible and immediate goal. In these manifestations—as I have earlier pointed out—the sixth ray influence can easily be seen. When, however, an individual sixth ray influence can be noted in an era wherein the sixth ray is uniquely active, then the reason for the potency of the religious idea, as expressed in theological dogma and doctrine and the universal authority of the Churches can be seen.

This orientation of man to the world of higher values has been the main objective of the Piscean age which is ending now and of the sixth ray influence which is so

rapidly passing out. Though there has never been a time
when this basic orientation has not been going steadily forward, it is of value to bear in mind that during the past
two thousand years a much higher, rarer and more difficult
process of orientation has been held before the race and
for the following reason. The fourth kingdom in nature
has been definitely attracted upwards towards the emerging
fifth kingdom and this has made necessary also the shift
of attention away from the three worlds of human endeavour and expression into the higher world of soul consciousness. It has necessitated likewise the refocussing of
the instinctual and intellectual attention which are the main
factors in the unfoldment of divine awareness. This awareness can be instinctual, intellectual and therefore human,
and also spiritual. But all three are equally divine, which
is a point oft forgotten.

The second objective of the sixth ray disciple or of the
man who is emerging out of the sixth ray influence but is
still conditioned by it (being a representative human being
from the current evolutionary angle) has been the unfolding
of the "capacity for abstraction," as it has been called. The
outstanding quality of our day and period, as a result of
transmuting human quality and character in and through
its disciples, has been the expression of the idealistic nature
of man, or of his instinctual response to the higher intuitional values. In the past, highly developed but rare people
have here and there demonstrated this power to abstract
the consciousness from the material or form side of life and
to focus it upon the ideal and upon the formless expression
of living truth. Today, whole masses of people and entire
nations are regimented to certain forms of idealism and
can and do appreciate ideas, formulated into ideals. Thus
again the success of the evolutionary process can be seen

and the work of the Hierarchy, as it endeavours to expand human consciousness, can be demonstrated to be effective.

Because of the potency of the sixth ray activity, owing to the long period wherein it has been expressing itself, the reaction of the average human being is one of an intense devotion to his own particular ideal, plus the effort, fanatically, to impose his idealistic dream (for that is all it potentially is) upon his fellowmen and to do so in such a form that unfortunately the original idea is lost, the primal ideal is destroyed and the devotee becomes much more occupied by the method of applying his ideal than by the ideal itself. Thus the idea is lost in the ideal and the ideal, in its turn, in the method of its application. The man becomes the devotee of an ideal which may or may not be embodied in an individual expression; this controls his thoughts, fore-ordains his activities and leads him frequently to merciless excesses in the interest of his peculiar and formulated idea.

Under the immediate expression of the sixth ray, the divine principle of desire has shifted potently away from the desire for material form into the realm of higher desire. Though materialism is still rampant, there are few people who are not animated by certain definite idealistic aspirations for which they are ready, when needed, to make sacrifices. This is a relatively new phenomenon and one that should be carefully noted. Down the ages, great sons of God have ever been ready to die for an idea; today, whole masses of men are equally ready and have done so, whether it is the idea of a superhuman state, empire or nation, or some response to a major world need, or some potent adherence to some current ideology. This indicates phenomenal racial achievement and the pronounced success of the Hierarchy to shift human attention into the world from whence ideas emerge and on to the higher and the less material values.

The instinct which has characterised this passing sixth ray period and which has been noticeably fostered under its influence is that of *taste*—taste in food, in human intercourse, in colour, in form, in art and architecture and in all branches of human knowledge. This discriminating taste has reached a relatively high stage of development during the past two thousand years and "good taste" is a highly cherished mass virtue and objective today. This is a totally new thing and one which has been hitherto the prerogative of the highly cultured few. Ponder on this. It connotes evolutionary achievement. For the disciples of the world, this sense of taste has to be transmuted into its higher correspondence—a discriminating sense of values. Hence the clear emphasis laid in all textbooks on discipleship upon the need to develop *discrimination*. Desire—taste—discrimination; these are the values, under the sixth ray, for all evolutionary unfoldment and peculiarly the goal of all disciples.

The methods whereby the activity of the sixth ray and its objectives have been imposed upon the race are three in number:

1. The development of instinct. This is followed by intelligently recognised desire and thus there is a steady expansion of requirements, of realisation and then of reorientation.

2. The consequent stimulation of the human consciousness towards expansion, leading finally to spiritual aspiration.

3. The reflection of reality in the mind consciousness follows next and this is sensed, demanded and sought through the medium of group work.

The apparatus of the human being, which is the mechanism whereby the soul contacts the three worlds which would be otherwise (under the present plan) sealed and hidden to the experience and experiment of the soul, has been more acutely sensitised and developed during the past two thousand years than in any previous period of ten thousand years. The reason for this is that the mind of man has been consciously aiding in the process of coordinating the instincts and transmuting instinctual reaction, translating it into intelligent perception. In the case of the world disciples, this process has been carried forward into the next stage of unfoldment to which we give the name of intuitional knowledge. The counterparts of the five senses and their higher correspondences upon the subtler planes are being rapidly unfolded, organised and recognised and it is by means of these inner senses that spiritual discovery becomes possible as well as the more familiar psychic discoveries. In the three phases:

    a. Instinct to aspiration
    b. Stimulation of divine desire
    c. The reflection of reality

you have the history of the activity of the sixth ray and of its relation during the past few centuries to its major field of expression, the astral plane.

We can now proceed to consider the seventh ray in its relation to the present situation in just the same way as we considered the sixth ray. Through doing this, there will unfold in your consciousness an idea of the developing process and of the emerging events and of the imminent happenings which may logically be expected. There are, as you may realise, two ways in which any particular ray may

be considered. It can be studied, first of all, from the angle
of energy which is ever coming into relation with other
energies and forces, producing through their meeting and
frequent conflict a situation entirely different and changed
from that which existed prior to the contact. The stages of
this import might be covered briefly by the following words:
Contact, conflict, adjustment, equilibrium (a form of stale-
mate or static condition such as was arrived at during the
19th century), absorption and the final disappearance of
the weaker outgoing energy. The conclusion is always inevitable for it is not the rays themselves which are in conflict but the substance and the forms which are implicated
during the period. Secondly: the quality of the ray can be
considered. This is in reality the expression of its soul and
intrinsic nature, which—impinging upon the condition existing when the ray comes into manifestation—definitely does
three things:

1. Changes the nature of the civilisation and the culture of
    humanity in any given period. It is this force which the
    Hierarchy utilises when any meeting of the ray energies
    takes place. The culture is first changed, because all
    basic quality changes work ever from above downwards,
    and it is the intelligentsia who are at first sensitive to
    the incoming differences. Form changes then auto-
    matically reverse the process. It is thus that points of
    juncture inevitably occur throughout the evolutionary
    process. When the scientists concerned with the theory
    and processes of evolution accept and study the ray pro-
    cedure, definite changes in attitude and a closer approach
    to the truth will at once appear. This concept also lies
    behind the teaching which I have given anent the Great
    Approaches which must take place (and can take place

very shortly) between the fourth and the fifth kingdoms in nature. Of the fifth kingdom, the Hierarchy is the dynamic and living nucleus.

2. Changes in the other kingdoms in nature, producing a different quality in the manifestation of the soul of any kingdom (for they all differ in soul quality) and consequently changes in the form aspect as well.

3. Changes in the type of egos or souls which will take incarnation during any particular ray period. By this I mean that just as during the age which is now coming to an end, the bulk of the incarnating souls were predominantly sixth ray in quality, so we can look for an increasing number of seventh ray egos now to appear. The furtherance of the coming seventh ray civilisation of synthesis, fusion, and of increased soul expression, and the development of the new stage into which the white magic of the Hierarchy is entering is, therefore, inevitable and for this stage there should be definite preparation and training.

The powers of the magical age are many and one of the reasons why the seventh ray is now making its appearance is that, owing to the rapid perfecting and integration of the human personality, the higher integration between soul and personality is today more possible and more easily accomplished than ever before. The new forms, through which that much desired consummation can be affected, must be consequently gradually and scientifically developed. This, as you may well conceive, will be achieved through the intensification of the forces, functioning through the etheric body, through the coordination of the seven major centres, and the establishing of their rhythmic relationship. The seventh ray governs predominantly upon the etheric levels of the physical plane. It does not govern the dense physical form which is under the control of the third ray. It is the vital or the etheric body which is responsive to and developed by the incoming seventh ray influences.

In considering the methods whereby the seventh ray purposes are achieved, I would like to point out that it is in this part of our discussion that I am limited and handicapped by language, because we are dealing with that which is new and, therefore, not as yet to be truly comprehended, and with those developments which will be eventually brought about by means of a true and scientific magic. This new magic will have no more relation to the crude attempts and oft ridiculous undertakings of the magicians, alchemists and performers of the past than c-a-t, cat, has to an algebraical formula. I would remind you also that in that home of ancient magic which you call Egypt, the magical work there performed was definitely concentrated upon the producing of physical effects and material results, and that the focus of the attention of the magician of the day can be seen in the stupendous production of those ancient and gigantic forms, standing silent and still in their pristine magnificence, which today call for the attention of archeologists and travellers; the forms of lesser magic which they produced were dedicated to the magical protection of the physical form and allied matters. In later days, we have the appearance of alchemy in its many forms plus its search for the Philosopher's Stone and the teaching as to the three basic mineral elements. They were driven esoterically and from the subjective side of life to search for that which could unify the three lower physical levels and this is in its nature deeply symbolic of racial unfoldment. These levels symbolise the integrated man—physical, astral and mental. When to these elements the Philosopher's Stone is added and has done its magical work, then you have the symbolic representation of the control by the soul of the four higher levels of the physical plane, the etheric or energy levels. Of this desirable consummation, the Philosopher's Stone is the emblem. I said "emblem," and I did not say "symbol." A symbol is an outer and visible sign of an inner and spiritual reality, carried out into expression upon the physical plane by the force of the inner embodied life. An emblem is man's formulation of a concept, created by man and embodying for him the truth as he sees it and understands it. A symbol is ever greater in its implications than is an emblem.

The etheric levels are also the field of expression for the soul, whether it is the human soul or the soul as an expression of the higher triad, the monadic life. I wonder whether any of you have the faintest idea what will happen to humanity when the inner subjective reality, functioning through the etheric body and pouring its forces unimpeded through the centres in that body, will have made its major controlling integration with the dense physical apparatus, reducing it to complete submission as a result of the higher integration, consummated between soul and personality.

We are, therefore, at a most interesting and crucial period in racial and planetary history—a period unlike any which has preceded it and for the reason that the evolutionary process has been definitely successful in spite of all failures, mistakes, and delays; of these latter there have been many owing to the refusal (curious and difficult to understand in your eyes) of the Energies, concentrated at Shamballa, to impose the force of will on matter and on form until such time as this can be done with the cooperation of the human family. This has never been possible hitherto, owing to the unpreparedness of man for the task and his ignorance as to the Plan. The Lord of Shamballa and His Helpers have had to wait until at least the dim outlines of the Plan had penetrated through into the consciousness of the race; this is beginning to happen with increasing frequency, and from day to day more and more intelligent men and women are coming (or are being brought) into touch with the emerging ideas of the Hierarchy. We can look, therefore, for the steady appearance, gradually and cautiously applied, of the will energy of the highest centre (Shamballa) which is to be found upon our planet. This centre corresponds to the monadic centre which makes its power felt in the consciousness of the disciple who is ready for the third initiation. Once the second initiation has been taken, the watching Hierarchy can begin to note the constant reorientation of the soul towards the monad and the attractive power of that highest aspect over the initiate. Today, so many members of the human family— in incarnation or out of incarnation—have taken the first two initiations that the attention of Shamballa is being increasingly turned to humanity, via the Hierarchy, whilst simultaneously the thoughts of men are being turned to the Plan, to the use of the will in direction and guidance, and to the nature of dynamic force. The quality, for instance of the explosive and dynamic nature of war in this century is indicative of this, for the will energy in one of its aspects is an expression of death and destruction; the first ray is the ray of the destroyer. What can, therefore, be seen occurring is the effect of the Shamballa force upon the forms in nature, due to the misuse of the incoming energy by man. War in the past, speaking generally and esoterically, has been based consistently upon the attractive power of possessions and this has led to the aggressive and grasping character of the motives which have led to war. Gradually there has been a change coming about and war has lately been founded upon somewhat higher motives and the acquisition of more land and territorial possessions has not been the true and the main motive. War has been prompted by economic necessity, or it has been in the nature of the imposition of the will of some nation or group of nations and their desire to impose some ideology or other upon some nation or to rid itself of a worn out system of thought, of government, of religious dogma which is holding back racial development. This is being now consciously done and is an expression of the Shamballa or will force and is not so definitely the desire force of the past.

The seventh ray is one of the direct lines along which this first ray energy can travel and here again is another reason for its appearance at this time, because, in the releasing of the life into the new and improved forms, the old ways of living, of culture and of civilisation have to be destroyed or modified. This is, all of it, the work of the first Ray of Will expressing itself predominantly at this present time through the seventh Ray of Organisation and Relationship.

When we studied the sixth ray, we considered first of all the effect of the ray upon the work and training, the life and the plans of the disciple, conditioning as it inevitably must his activities and life output. Then we considered the motivating principle of desire in this connection and finally touched upon the three modes of the prevalent ray activity. Let us follow the same procedure now, thus gaining some idea of the relationship between the sixth and the seventh rays and the manner in which the potency of the sixth ray has prepared humanity for the imminent happenings with which it is faced.

What I have now to say will not be followed with ease

or with due appreciation by the sixth ray disciple, because the methods employed by Those Who are handling and directing the new energies are not comprehensible by him, grounded as he is in the methods of the past; hence the appearance of the fundamentalist schools, found in every field of thought—religious, political and even scientific. Again, when the sixth ray disciple attempts to use the new incoming energies, they express themselves for him upon the astral plane and the result is astral magic, deepened glamour and pronounced deception. To this fact must be ascribed today the appearance of teachers, claiming to teach magic, to bring about certain magical results, to work with rays of differing colours and to utilise Words of Power, to pronounce decrees and to be repositories of the hitherto unrevealed wishes and secrets of the Masters of the Wisdom. It is all a form of astral glamour, and the contacting upon the astral plane of that which will later precipitate upon earth. But the time is not yet and the hour for such usages has not arrived. The sense of time and the understanding of the correct hour for the carrying out of the Plan in its future detail has not been learnt by these sincere, but deluded, people and—focussed as they are upon the astral plane and undeveloped as they are mentally—they misinterpret to themselves and for others that which they there psychically sense. They know far too little and yet believe that they know much. They speak with authority, but it is the authority of the unexpanded mind. The expression of old magical patterns, the digging up of hints and indications of crystallised and worn-out methods from the ancient past is all too prevalent at this time and is responsible for much deception of the masses and consequent mass delusion.

White magic—as I would have you remember—is concerned with the unfoldment of the soul in form and its gaining needed experience thereby. It is not concerned with direct work upon the form but with the indirect influence of the soul, functioning in any form in every kingdom in nature as it brings the form under its control, thereby effecting needed and developing changes in the apparatus of contact. The white magician knows that when the proper and correct ray stimulation is applied to the centre which we call the soul in any form but not to the form itself, that then the soul, thus stimulated, will do its own work of destruction, of attraction, of rebuilding and of a consequent renewed life manifestation. This is true of the soul of man, of the soul of a nation and of the soul of humanity itself. Bear this in mind, for I have here stated a basic and fundamental rule by which all white magic is agelessly governed.

It is for this reason that the seventh ray is spoken of as governing the mineral kingdom and also as manifesting through its mediumship that significant soul characteristic and quality which we call *radiation*. That word effectively describes the result of soul stimulation upon and within every form. The life of the soul eventually radiates beyond the form and this radiation produces definite and calculated effects. The sixth ray is, as you know, very closely related to the animal kingdom and its effect there is to produce in the higher forms of animal life the quality and expression of domesticity, and the adaptability of the animal to human contact. The rays controlling the animal kingdom are the seventh, the third and the sixth. Hence you can easily see that the relation which exists between the higher animals and man is a ray relation and, therefore, useful under the evolutionary law and inevitable in its results. The rays governing the vegetable kingdom are the sixth, the second and the fourth and here again there is an interlocking relation through the medium of the sixth ray. The human kingdom is governed by the fourth, the fifth and again the fourth and this again indicates relationship. Some day these relations and inter-connected lines of force will be better understood and scientifically studied and the lines of related energies investigated. This interlocking directorate of energies will engage the attention of some of the best minds and when that takes place much will be learnt. This information is, however, of negligible use at this time and will remain so until such time as men are sensitive to the vibration of the different rays and can isolate a ray rhythm in their consciousness. When this sensitivity is developed, then many rapid, significant and revolutionary discoveries will be made.

One of the inevitable effects of seventh ray energy will be to relate and weld into a closer synthesis the four kingdoms in nature. This must be done as preparatory to the long fore-ordained work of humanity which is to be the distributing agency for spiritual energy to the three subhuman kingdoms. This is the major task of service which the fourth kingdom, through its incarnating souls, has undertaken. The radiation from the fourth kingdom will some day be so potent and far-reaching that its effects will permeate down into the very depths of the created phenomenal world, even into the mineral kingdom. Then we shall see the results to which the great initiate, Paul, refers when he speaks of the whole creation waiting for the manifestation of the Sons of God. That manifestation is that of radiating glory and power and love.

Incidentally I might point out here that the seventh ray influence will have three definite effects upon the fourth and third kingdoms in nature. These are as follows:

1. All animal bodies will be steadily refined and in the case of humanity consciously refined, and so brought to a higher and more specialised state of development. This is today proceeding with rapidity. Diet and athletics, open air and sunshine are doing much for the race and in the next two generations fine bodies and sensitive natures will make their appearance and the soul will have far better instruments through which to work.

2. The relation between the human and the animal kingdoms will become increasingly close. The service of the animal to man is well recognised and of ceaseless expression. The service of man to the animals is not yet understood though some steps in the right direction are being taken. There must eventually be a close synthesis and sympathetic coordination between them and when this is the case some very extraordinary occurrences of animal mediumship under human inspiration will take place. By means of this, the intelligent factor in the animal (of which instinct is the embryonic manifestation) will be rapidly developed and this is one of the outstanding results of the intended human-animal relationship.

3. There will be, as a consequence of this quickened evolution, the rapid destruction of certain types of animal bodies. Very low grade human bodies will disappear, causing a general shift in the racial types towards a higher standard. Many species of animals will also die out and are today disappearing, and hence the increasing emphasis upon the preservation of animals and the establishing of game preserves.

In this comparative, even if inadequate, study of the old and of the new types of discipleship, one of the problems facing the Hierarchy is how to bring about the necessary changes in technique and method of development which the seventh ray type will require and yet at the same time so condition these changes that there can be smooth process of adjustment and interplay between the Hierarchy and the world aspirants. This adjustment must include the two groups (one at present large and the other still small) of sixth and seventh ray disciples. The problems of the Hierarchy are, of course, no real concern of those who have not achieved liberation and cannot, therefore, look at life through the eyes of those who are no longer held by the forces of the three worlds, but it might serve a useful purpose if disciples occasionally gave some thought to the relation as it exists upon the Masters' side and gave less thought to their own individual and peculiar difficulties.

One of the major characteristics of the seventh ray disciple is his intense practicality. He works upon the physical plane with a constant and steady objective in order to bring about results which will be effective in determining the forms of the coming culture and civilisation; towards the end of the seventh ray cycle he will work equally hard to perpetuate what he has brought about. He wields force in order to build the forms which will meet his requirements and does this more scientifically than do disciples on other rays. The sixth ray devotee is far more abstract and mystical in his work and thought, and seldom has any real understanding of the right relation between form and energy. He thinks almost entirely in terms of quality and pays little attention to the material side of life and the true significance of substance as it produces phenomena. He is apt to regard matter as evil in nature and form as a limitation, and only lays the emphasis upon soul consciousness as of true importance. It is this failure to work intelligently, and I would like to add, lovingly with substance and so bring it into right relation with the dense outer form that has made the last two thousand years produce so disastrously a mismanaged world and which has brought the population of the planet into its present serious condition. The unintelligent work upon the physical plane, carried forward by those influenced by the sixth ray force, has led to a world which is suffering from cleavage in as true a sense as an individual person can suffer from a "split personality." The lines of demarcation between science and religion are a striking instance of this and have been clearly and forcefully drawn. The cleavage to which I refer has been drawn by the churchmen of the past and by no one else; the lines have been determined by the mystics, impractical and visionary, and by the fanatical devotees of some idea who were, nevertheless, unable to see the broad implications and the universal nature of these recognised ideas. I am generalising. There have been many devoted and holy sons of God who have never been guilty of the above stupidities and separative tendencies. At the same time as we recognise this, we must also recognise that orthodox religion has temporarily separated the two great concepts of spirit and matter in their thought and teaching, thereby pushing apart religion and science.

The task of the new age workers is to bring these two apparent opposites together, to demonstrate that spirit and matter are not antagonistic to each other and that throughout the universe there is only spiritual substance, working on and producing the outer tangible forms.

When a form and an activity is what you call evil, it is only so because the motivating energy behind the form and responsible for the activity is wrongly oriented, selfishly impulsed and incorrectly used. Here again the two basic truisms of modern occultism (there are others which will be imparted when these two are mastered and rightly applied) are of importance:

1. Energy follows thought.
2. Right motive creates right action and right forms.

These two statements are of very ancient origin but are as yet but little understood. Hence the first thing which every disciple has to learn is the nature, control and direction of energy; he does this by working with initiating causes, by learning the nature of the realm of causes and by developing the capacity to get behind the effect to the cause which generated or produced it. In the case of the individual disciple and in the preliminary stage of his training, this involves the constant investigation of his motives until he has discovered what they are and has so directed his thought that those motives can, in every case, be depended upon to work automatically and dynamically under soul direction.

The sixth ray disciple, in the majority of cases, carries his work down as far as the astral plane and there lies the focus of his attention, his life and his thought. Automatically and of necessity, his physical nature responds to the impulse sent from the astral plane, motivated from the mental and—at times—directed by the soul. But the potency of this desire and his determination to see the fruit of his labour has produced much difficulty in the past by arresting the true expression of the originating impulse. It is arrested upon the astral plane. This has been balanced by the cyclic intervention of other ray forces or otherwise the situation would be much worse than it is. The seventh ray disciple will bring the energy which he is wielding right down on to the physical plane, thereby producing integration; and the dualism which characterises it will be that of a centre of energy upon the mental plane and one upon the physical plane. The dualism of the sixth ray worker is that of the pairs of opposites upon the astral plane.

It will be apparent, therefore, that, having established the two points of energy (mental and physical), the next task of the worker in magic will be to produce a synthesis upon the physical plane of the available energies, to concretise them, and invest that which has been constructed with the potency of activity and persistence. The energy thus employed will, in the majority of cases, be of three kinds:

1. The energy of the mind. This will be the dominant controlling energy used during the period of accepted discipleship and until the second initiation.
2. The energy of the soul. This will be wielded, used and creatively employed from the second until the third initiation.
3. The energy of soul and mind, blended and synthesised. This combination is of tremendous potency. After the fourth initiation, this will be augmented by energy coming from the Monad.

I would have you bear in mind that, though all is energy yet at the same time in correct esoteric teaching the higher impulsive activity is called *energy* and that which is conditioned by and swept into activity through its agency is called *force*. The terms are therefore relative and movable. For the bulk of humanity, for instance, astral impulse is the highest energy to which they normally aspire and the forces upon which astral energy plays will then be the etheric and physical forces. Higher energies may intermittently control, but as a general rule the life incentive or impulse is astral, and this can either be called desire or aspiration, according to the objective. The latter may simply be mental ambition or desire for power and the term "aspiration" should not be confined only to so-called religious impulses, mystical longings and the demand for liberation.

The seventh ray disciple works consciously by means of certain laws, which are the laws governing form and its relation to spirit or life. In *A Treatise on Cosmic Fire*, I gave you the three major laws of the solar system and the seven subsidiary laws through which these three express themselves; I gave you also indications as to the laws which govern group work. You must remember that disciples upon different rays will wield these laws according to the quality of their ray impulses (I am handicapped here for words which are appropriate), interpreting them in terms of their specific life obligation or dharma and producing the desired results through the medium of differing ray techniques, conforming always, however, to the inevitability of the results wrought by the energies which they have released to play upon forces under the laws of their being. The sixth ray disciple, working with the laws of nature and of the soul, will qualify his results and produce his creative forms upon the astral plane; he has consequently to learn frequently to work through a seventh ray personality for several lives (either before or after achieving discipleship) before he will be able to bring through on to the physical plane his dream and his vision. The seventh ray disciple has no such problem. By his knowledge of ritual (which is the ancient codified means whereby the attractive and expressive nature of the energies to be employed are organised and related), by his understanding of the "Words of Power" (which he discovers by experiment) and by using the potency of sound, the disciple of the future will work and build the new world with its culture and civilisation. A curious indication of the effect of the seventh ray magical work upon the mass consciousness is the growing use of slogans and of "catch phrases" (is that not the term used?) which are employed to bring about results and to sweep human beings into certain forms of mass action. This is the embryonic use of Words of Power, and from a study of their tonal values, their numerological indications and their inherent potency, men will eventually arrive at vast magical achievements and creations, producing group activity and the appearance of certain forms of expression upon the outer plane. After all, scientific formulas have reduced the most intricate and abstruse discoveries to a few signs and symbols. The next step is to embody these signs and symbols into a word or words, thus imparting to them what is esoterically called "the power of embodiment." If I might express it this way, the ancient statement that "God spoke and the world were made" simply means that God's formula for creation was reduced to a great Word which He sounded forth and the inevitable results followed. Something of this process on a tiny human scale will be seen happening in the coming age. At present, what I have said above may sound fanciful and fantastic to the average student.

It will be obvious to you that seventh ray disciples wield much power and for this reason the emphasis in all teaching given to them is laid upon *purity of motive*. In the past, the emphasis has been laid upon *purity of body* in the case of the sixth ray disciples. As was inevitable, they have carried the idea to a fanatical extent, and have stressed celibacy, asceticism and stringent rules of physical life, oft making sinful that which is natural. This has been a necessary stage in their development for it was essential that the physical plane should become a greater factor in their consciousness and that their attention should be turned from the realm of abstraction (which is their line of least resistance) and focussed upon physical living, for, again, energy follows thought. Thus their attitude to life could become more practical and the necessary integration take place. Disciples in the new age will lay the emphasis upon the mental principle, because it conditions thought and speech. All magical work is based upon the energy of thought and of the spoken word (the expression of the two magical centres referred to above) and purity in the realm of the mind and motive is regarded consequently as a basic essential.

The seventh ray influence is that which will produce in a peculiar and unexpected sense the Western School of Occultism just as the sixth ray impulse has produced the Eastern School of Occultism—the latter bringing the light down on to the astral plane and the new incoming influence carrying it down on to the physical. The Eastern teaching affected Christianity and indicated and determined the lines of its development and Christianity is definitely a bridging religion. The roles will eventually be reversed and the shift of the "light in the East" will be over Europe and America. This will inevitably bring about the needed and desired synthesis of the mystical way and the occult path. It will lead later to the formulation of the *higher way*; of this it is useless to speak at this time for you would not comprehend. None of the foundational and ancient *Rules of the Road* will ever be abrogated or discarded. Just as men used to travel on the ancient highways on foot, conforming to the requirement of their time and age, and today travel by rail or automobile (arriving at the same destination) so the same road will be followed, the same goal achieved but there may be different procedures, varying safeguards and changed protective measures. The rules may vary from time to time in order to provide easier indi cation and adequate protection. The training of the disciple in the future will differ in detail from that of the past but the basic rules remain authoritative.

The keynote, governing the development of the sixth ray disciple, was expressed for him in the words of Christ when He said: "I, if I be lifted up, will draw all men." The emphasis of all sixth ray work is Attraction and Repulsion—hence division and cleavage, producing eventually a realisation of the necessity for a consciously undertaken synthesis and integration, mentally motivated and produced. The history of Christianity (which is the history of Europe) will stand illumined if the Law of Attraction and Repulsion is studied in connection with its eventful past. The use and misuse of this law and its constant interpretations in terms of material desires, personal ambitions, and territorial control produced the many schisms and cleavages and will account for much that happened. Under the seventh ray influence, these cleavages will end and synthesis will eventually take place.

The keynote of the seventh ray disciple is "Radiatory Activity." Hence the emergence in world thought of certain new ideas—mental radiation or telepathy, the radiatory use of heat, the discovery of radium. All this connotes seventh ray activity.

The divine principle with which the seventh ray humanity will be mainly concerned is that of life as it expresses itself through the medium of the etheric body. It is for this reason that we find a growing interest in the nature of vitality; the function of the glands is being studied and before long their major function as vitality generators will be noted. Esoterically, they are regarded as externalisations upon the physical plane of the force centres in the etheric body and their aliveness or their lack of activity are indicative of the condition of those centres. The shift of the world interest is also into the realm of economics which is definitely the realm of life sustenance. Much is, therefore, bound to happen in all these spheres of interest, and once the etheric body becomes an established scientific fact and the centres— major and minor—are recognised as the foci of all energy as it expresses itself through the human body upon the physical plane, we shall see a great revolution take place in medicine, in diet and in the handling of daily life activity. This will produce great changes in the mode of work and labour and above everything else in the leisure activities of the race.

This thought brings to our attention the three methods of activity as employed by all the ray workers and which differ for each ray. Those which will eventually control the seventh ray types will gradually bring about changed attitudes to life and very different methods of daily living. These three are:

1. Group activity for the scientific relation of substance and energy.
2. The stimulation of etheric forms through rightly directed force.
3. The correct distribution, through scientific study, of vital energy.

We are entering a scientific age, but it will be a science which passes out of the impasse which it has now reached and which—having penetrated as it has into the realm of the intangible—will begin to work far more subjectively than heretofore. It will recognise the existence of senses which are super-sensory and which are extensions of the five physical senses, and this will be forced upon science because of the multitude of reliable people who will possess them and who can work and live in the worlds of the tangible and the intangible simultaneously. The mass of reputable testimony will prove incontrovertible. The moment that the subjective world of causes is proven to exist (and this will come through the indisputable evidence of man's extended senses) science will enter into a new era; its focus of attention will change; the possibilities of discovery will be immense and materialism (as that word is now understood) will vanish. Even the word "materialism" will become obsolete and men in the future will be amused at the limited vision of our modern world and wonder why we thought and felt as we did.

I would have you bear in mind in connection with the five rays which we have seen are influencing or beginning to influence humanity at this time (the first, second, third, sixth and seventh rays) that their effect varies according to the ray type or ray quality of the individual concerned and according to his position upon the ladder of evolution. Such points are often forgotten. If a man is, for instance, upon the second Ray of Love-Wisdom, it may be expected that the influence of that ray and of the sixth (which is along the second ray line of power) will be easily effective and will necessarily constitute the line of least resistance. This situation may, therefore, produce undue sensitivity and an unbalanced unfoldment of characteristics. It is our characteristics which influence our conduct and our reactions to circumstance. It will mean also that the influence of the first, third and seventh rays will be fundamentally unsettling and will call out resistance or—at the very least—an attitude of non-receptivity. In the world today, the rays which are along the line of energy which is that of the first Ray of Will or Power (including the third and the seventh) are in the ratio of three to two (as regards present manifestation) and, therefore, we can look for a fuller expression of the first ray attributes and happenings than would otherwise be the case. This will be particularly so because the sixth ray is fast going out of manifestation. All the above constitutes a piece of information which is of small value at this time. Its implications will become increasingly apparent as time goes on and I am, therefore, including them in my teaching.

7. *Initiation in the Aquarian Age.*

I have hinted at the orientation which has been or will be carried out in connection with the three major world centres; I have also hinted at the relation of certain of the major initiations to these centres. These hints constitute a new line of thought. In this connection there are one or two points which I would like to develop in connection with this, so as to make the entire subject considerably clearer than it is at present. I would like also to relate these centres to the rays which are now in manifestation (either coming in, passing out or in full expression). Speaking with brevity, we could say that:

The first initiation is closely related to the planetary centre which is humanity itself. It will produce, when over, an increased stimulation of the intellect as it expresses itself as ordered activity upon the physical plane. It is also closely connected with the third Ray of Active Intelligence. This third ray has been in objective manifestation since 1425 A.D. and will remain in incarnation throughout the Aquarian Age. Its cycles are the longest of any of the ray cycles. However, within these major cycles there are periods of intensified activity which are like the beat or pulsation of the heart and these periods last approximately three thousand years. They are, when out of incarnation, called "cycles of withdrawal but not of abstraction." They are three thousand years also in incarnation. One of these three thousand year periods of expression is now here and we can look for much development of the intellectual faculty and a marked increase of creative work during this time. This particular cycle of expression marks a climaxing point in the larger cycle. During the coming age, the intelligence of the race and its active development will assume real proportions and this with much speed.

The intensification of the life of the human centre will proceed apace and this is the reason why so many people (as I have earlier hinted) will take the first initiation. Students are apt to forget that the first initiation can be described, in reality as:

a. The grounding or externalisation of the Christ principle in humanity as a whole and upon the physical plane.

b. The flowering of the intelligence so that the initiate can work powerfully upon the mental plane and humanity itself be lifted up and aided throughout every part thereby.

c. The coming into activity of the throat centre and (because the third ray is closely connected with the first ray) the first faint orientation of the spiritual man towards Shamballa can take place, becoming more and more intensified and pronounced at the time of the third initiation. I would like here to point out the numerical correspondences:

1. The third great world centre—humanity.
2. The activity of the third ray—active intellect.
3. The third initiation which marks the consummation of the 1st, just as the 4th initiation marks the consummation of the second, and the fifth of the third.

4. The third major centre—the throat centre.
5. The third race—the Aryan, as it expresses the first strictly human race, the Lemurian.
6. The third plane—the physical, the reflection of the third highest plane, the atmic.
7. The third periodical vehicle—the personality.
8. The third divine aspect—intelligence.
9. The third grade of divine messenger—Hercules.
10. The sustaining Life, the third or outer Sun—the physical sun.

These are a few of the correspondences which it is helpful for us to bear in mind in so far as they reveal divine quality, spiritual intent and universal objectives.

During the Aquarian Age and during one third of its expression, that is, during the first decanate, esoterically considered, the vitalising of the human centre (spiritually considered) and in relation to the Plan and the steady growth of widespread creative activity, both in the individual and the race, will be increasingly seen. This will be due to the work and influence of Saturn, which is governed by the third ray. This planet is the planet of opportunity, of discipleship and of testing and the race can look for an increasing expression of Saturnian activity as that great divine Life continues His beneficent task.

The second initiation is closely related to the Hierarchy as a planetary centre and to the activity of the second ray. This initiation will produce in the initiate a growing sense of relationships, of a basic unity with all that breathes, and a recognition of the One Life which will lead eventually to that state of expressed brotherhood which it is the goal of the Aquarian Age to bring into being. This major centre, the Hierarchy, brings to bear upon humanity the focussed life of love and it is this basic love which the second deca-nate of Aquarius—governed as it is by Mercury—will bring into manifestation. Mercury, the Messenger of the Gods (that is, of the Hierarchy of souls), carries always the mes-sage of love and sets up an unbreakable inter-relation between the two great planetary centres, that of the Hier-archy and that of Humanity.

You have again in this connection certain fundamental numerical correspondences, which are based upon the com-ing into activity of an awakened heart centre in the race. This is the second major centre in the individual and is situated above the diaphragm, and through it the Hierarchy can reach the whole of humanity and the subhuman king-doms likewise.

1. The second planetary centre—the Hierarchy.
2. The activity of the second ray—love-wisdom.
3. The second initiation, which relates the solar plexus to the heart, humanity to the Hierarchy and the per-sonality and the egoic rays to the second, which is ever basically in manifestation.
4. The second ray centre—heart centre.
5. The second race (the Atlantean) as it climaxes in the fourth, the next race.
6. The second plane—the astral plane. This is the reflec-tion of the second highest plane.
7. The second periodical vehicle—the soul.
8. The second divine aspect—love-wisdom.
9. The second type or grade of Messenger—Christ. Buddha.
10. The sustaining Life, the second or subjective Sun—heart of sun.

To all these is related the sixth ray as allied to or subsidiary to the second.

In this world cycle it might be said that the emphasis of all spiritual power is placed in the Hierarchy which is, at present, the divine intermediary, interpreting the will of God, which is the purpose of Shamballa. It transmits or steps down the divine energy so that safe application to Humanity becomes possible. It will be apparent, therefore, why in the second decanate of Aquarius the Hierarchy can, as the representative of Shamballa and with the aid of Mercury, bring into physical manifestation the coming Avatar. This becomes possible when the work of the first decanate is accomplished and when Shamballa has released and definitely re-oriented the energies of the third great centre, that of Humanity. This release and readjustment leads to creative expression and renewed spiritual life. Planetary alignment can take place and this is a planned objective for which the Hierarchy is preparing and for which the Avatar Himself is preparing at Shamballa.

The third initiation is connected with Shamballa as a planetary centre and to the activity of the first ray. It should be borne in mind that this is the *first* initiation in which personality and soul are united and fused so that the two aspects form one unit. When this initiation has taken place, it happens that for the first time some of its broader group implications become a reality and henceforth constitute the motivating impulse of the initiate's life. Aspiration ends and the intensest conviction takes its place. It is interesting also to note that Venus now comes into control in the third decanate of the Aquarian Age. Venus is esoterically recognised as that mysterious force which is a blend of love and knowledge, of intelligence and synthesis, and of understanding and brotherhood. Within the Hierarchy itself, the two great Messengers who have embodied the dual Venusian energy were the Buddha and the Christ. The Messenger Who will later come and express the Shamballa urge to synthesis, the hierarchial aspiration towards love and the desire of humanity for intelligent activity with combined power will gather all into Himself. All these qualities will focus in Him, plus another quality or divine principle of which the race of men as yet knows nothing and for which there is, as yet, no name. He will be a great and potent Avatar and is not along the line of our humanity at all.

The numerical correspondences might be noted as follows, remembering that the third initiation is, in reality, the first initiation of the soul, after complete identification with the personality within the life and consciousness of the Monad, the One and the First.

1. The first planetary centre—Shamballa.
2. The activity of the first ray—will or power.
3. The third initiation which is the first soul initiation, relating the base of the spine to the head centre, and the soul to the Monad.
4. The first major centre—the head.
5. The first truly divine race—the final race.
6. The third plane, which is in reality the first plane of soul consciousness, the reflection of the highest plane, the Logoic.
7. The first periodical vehicle—the monadic.
8. The first divine aspect—will or power.
9. The first or highest type of Mediator—the coming Avatar.
10. The sustaining Life, the spiritual sun—the central spiritual sun.

We will now consider the trend of the times and seasons as far as the rays are concerned:

RAY I—This ray is still out of physical manifestation but is beginning to have a definite effect upon the mental plane; there it influences the minds of disciples everywhere and lays the stage for the appearance of a certain group of disciples from Shamballa. Two thousand years from today, the influence of this ray will be felt powerfully upon the physical plane. One hundred years hence its potency will be noted upon the astral plane.

RAY II—This ray is always in subjective manifestation and very potent because it is the ray of our solar system and particularly so at this time as the Hierarchy is approaching closer to humanity in preparation for the "crisis of love," and an imminent major planetary initiation. At this time, however, the second ray is becoming objective in its influence upon the physical plane. It will become increasingly so for the next two thousand two hundred years when it will gradually withdraw into the background.

RAY III—This ray will remain in objective incarnation from the point of view of humanity for a very long time—so long a time that it is needless for us to anticipate its waning influence. That planetary centre which is Humanity itself still needs the intensified application of these forces so as to stimulate even the "lowest of the sons of men."

RAY IV—This ray, as you know, begins to come into incarnation early in the next century and—in collaboration with the developing Saturnian influence—will lead many on to the path of discipleship. When the peculiar energy to which we give the somewhat unsatisfactory name of "harmony through conflict" and the forces of that planet which stage opportunity for the aspirant are working in combination and an ordained synthesis, we can then look for a very rapid adjustment in human affairs, particularly in connection with the Path. This fourth ray is, in the last analysis, the ray which teaches the art of living in order to produce a synthesis of beauty. There is no beauty without unity, without embodied idealism and the resultant symmetrical unfoldment. This ray is *not* the ray of art, as it is often claimed, but is the energy which brings about the beauty of those living forms which embody the ideas and the ideals which are seeking immediate expression. Many people claim to be on the fourth ray because they dream of the artistic expressive life. As I have told you before, creative art expresses itself upon all the rays.

RAY V—This ray has been in manifestation for nearly seventy years. It will pass out (by special and unique arrangement) in another fifty years, thus breaking into its own normal cycle, because it is deemed that the needed special impulse has been adequate and that the impetus given to the human "spirit of discovery" has served its purpose. Any further intensification of the mental processes just now (except through the general pervasive effect of the third ray) might prove disastrous. The ray cycles are usually set and determined, but, in collaboration with each other and because of the imminent spiritual Crisis of Approach, the Lord of the Fifth Ray and the Lord of the World have decided temporarily to withdraw this type of force. It will take about fifty years to do this.

RAY VI—This ray has been passing out of manifestation for quite some time now, as you know, and will do so with increasing rapidity.

RAY VII—This ray is coming into effective expression now; there is little need for me to add here anything further to the mass of information which I have given you in this treatise and in my other books.

One small point of interest but one of no especial moment to you is that the Lords of the Rays, through Their planetary Representatives, constitute a body of directing Forces in collaboration with the Lord of the World at Shamballa. Their capacity is advisory and directive but not authoritative. This may be regarded by some of you as the most interesting piece of information in this book. If this is your attitude, then it only indicates your unpreparedness for true esoteric teaching. Students need a greater sense of the real governing values and a sense of spiritual proportion. Planetary facts and solar facts (under which heading the above item of information might well be placed) can stimulate your imagination and widen your horizon; for aspirants and disciples, that is the major value. All information and happenings which are connected with Shamballa are always exciting to the neophyte who is apt to forget that he must make his contact with the more familiar Hierarchy before true and related perception is his.

I would have you study the tabulation which I gave you in *Initiation, Human and Solar,* and which you will find in the appendix to the first volume of *A Treatise on the Seven Rays.* I insert it here for the benefit of those who have no copy of the first volume of the Treatise, and whose attention should be turned again from the magnitude of the Macrocosm to the responsibility of the microcosm.

DISCIPLESHIP AND THE RAYS

Ray I—Force—Energy—Action—The Occultist.

Ray II—Consciousness—Expansion—Initiation—The true Psychic.

Ray III—Adaptation—Development—Evolution—The Magician.

Ray IV—Vibration—Response—Expression—The Artist.

Ray V—Mentation—Knowledge—Science—The Scientist.

Ray VI—Devotion—Abstraction—Idealism—The Devotee.

Ray VII—Incantation—Magic—Ritual—The Ritualist.

In the Aquarian Age, as a result of the existing combination of ray influences, humanity enters into an expansion of consciousness which will reveal to him group relations instead of his individual and self-centered personal relations. I would remind you that Aquarius is to be found in the upper half of the zodiacal circle and is exactly opposite to Leo which is found in the lower half. Leo is the sign of individual unfoldment and of the self as self-assertive. This highly individualised sign consummates in Aquarius wherein the individual finds full expression through the medium of the group, passing from service to himself and expression of himself as a personality to service of the group and a growing expression of the Hierarchy to which he steadily draws closer. To this end, the ray influences will increasingly and steadily be directed. Humanity has reached a stage where the sense of individuality is rapidly emerging. In every field of human expression, men and women are becoming definitely self-assertive. The *Old Commentary* refers symbolically to this in the following words:

"The Lion begins to roar. He rushes forth and, in his urge to live, he wields destruction. And then again he roars and—rushing to the stream of life—drinks deep. Then, having drunk, the magic of the waters works. He stands transformed. The Lion disappears and he who bears the water pot stands forth and starts upon his mission."

Those with vision can see this happening upon every side today. The water-carrier (another name for the world server) is starting upon his self-appointed task. Hence the anchoring upon earth of the New Group of World Servers, whose representatives are found in every land and in every great city. This, I would remind you, has taken place without exception in every land and they work on all the different rays; they express many points of view; their field of service is widely differing and their techniques so diverse that in some cases comprehension is not easy to the smaller minded person. But, they all carry the pitcher containing the water of life upon their shoulder, reverting to the language of symbolism, and they all emit the light in some degree throughout their environment.

To you, who live and work in this interim period and in this cycle of transition, with all its resultant outer chaos and upheaval, is given the task of expressing steadfastness, service and sacrifice. Those are the three words which I give you. I have no spectacular information to give you, as has sometimes been the case. Too much of this engrossing and novel information can lead to deep-seated insensitiveness. You need to absorb and to act upon the information you already have, before there is evoked from you that basic demand for further light which necessitates response from those of us who work within the limits of the Hierarchy. For that demand, we patiently wait.

8. *Christ and the Coming New Age.*

As we come to an end of our consideration of the world today and its dominating rays, working through the nations and conditioning the people, there is a final point which I would like to make; it lies in the realm of religion and concerns the significance of Christmas. From the very night of time, as well you know, the period wherein the sun moves northward again has been regarded as a festival season; for thousands of years it has been associated with the coming of the Sun-God to save the world, to bring light and fruitfulness to the Earth and through the work of the Son of God to bring hope to humanity. The Christmas season is regarded by those who do not know any better as uniquely the Festival of the Christ, and this the Christian churches have emphasised and to this all churchmen testify. This is both true and false. The Founder of the Christian Church—God in the flesh—availed Himself of this period and came to us in the dark of the year and initiated a new era in which *light* was to be the distinguishing note. This has been true from several angles, even from the purely physical, for today we have a lighted world; everywhere lights are to be seen and the pitch dark nights of olden times are fast disappearing. Light has also descended on the earth in the form of the "light of knowledge." Today, education whose objective is to lead all men on to a "lighted way," is the keynote of our civilisation and is a major pre-occupation in all countries. The removal of illiteracy, the development of a true culture and the ascertaining of truth in all fields of thought and of research are of paramount importance in all lands.

Thus, when Christ proclaimed (as He assuredly did), along with all world Saviours and Sun-Gods, that He was

the Light of the worlds, He inaugurated a marvellous period
in which humanity has been widely and universally enlightened. This period dates from Christmas Day, two
thousand years ago, in Palestine. That was the greatest
of all Christmas Days and its emanating influence was more
potent than was any previous arrival of a Bearer of Light
because humanity was more ready for the light. Christ came
in the sign of Pisces, the Fishes—the sign of the divine
Intermediary in the highest sense, or of the medium in
the lower; it is the sign of many of the world Saviours and
of those Revealers of divinity Who establish world relationships. I would have you note that phrase. The major
impulse driving the Christ towards special work was the
desire to establish right human relations; it is also the
desire—realised or unrealised—of humanity, and we know
that some day the Desire of all nations will come, that
right human relations will be found everywhere and that
goodwill will implement that fulfilment, leading to peace
in all lands and among all peoples.

Down through the ages, Christmas Day has been recognised and kept as a season of new beginnings, of better
human contacts and of happier relations among families
and communities. Yet just as the churches have descended
into a profoundly materialistic presentation of Christianity
so the simple Christmas Day which would have pleased the
heart of Christ has degenerated into an orgy of spending,
of acquiring good things, and is regarded as a period which
is "good for trade." We need, therefore, to remember
that when any phase of life-inspired religion is interpreted
entirely materially, when any civilisation and culture loses
its sense of spiritual values and responds mainly to the
material values, then it has served its usefulness and must

pass away, and this in the interests of life itself and progress.

The message of the birth of Christ rings ever new but is not today understood. The emphasis during the Aquarian Age, the age into which we are fast entering, will shift away from Bethlehem to Jerusalem, and from the infant Saviour to the Risen Christ. Pisces has seen, during two thousand years, the spreading light; Aquarius will see the Rising Light, and of both of these the Christ is the eternal symbol.

The ancient story of the Birth will become universalised and be seen as the story of every disciple and initiate who takes the first initiation and in his time and place becomes a server and a lightbearer. In the Aquarian Age two momentous developments will take place:

1. The Birth Initiation will condition human thinking and aspiration everywhere.
2. The religion of the Risen Christ, and not of the newly born Christ or of the crucified Christ, will be the distinctive keynote.

It is seldom realised that hundreds of thousands of people in every land have taken, or are preparing to take, this first initiation, called the Birth at Bethlehem, the House of Bread. Humanity, the world disciple, is now ready for this. Indications of the accuracy of the above statement can be seen in the re-orientation of people everywhere to things spiritual, their interest in human good and human welfare, the perseverance they show in their search for light and their longing and desire for a true peace, based on right human relations, implemented by goodwill. This "mind as it is in Christ" can be seen in their revolt against materialistic religion and in the widespread effort to be seen in Europe and elsewhere to return the land (Mother-Earth, the true Virgin Mary) to the people. It can be seen in the constant movement of people throughout the world from place to place, symbolised in the Gospel story by the journey of Mary with the infant Jesus into Egypt.

Then followed, as we are told in the New Testament, a cycle of thirty years wherein all we know is that the infant Jesus grew to manhood and could then take the second initiation, the Baptism in Jordan, and begin His public service. Today the many who in this life have taken the first initiation are entering the long silence of that symbolic thirty years wherein they too will grow to manhood and take the second initiation. This initiation demonstrates the complete control of the emotional nature and of all Piscean characteristics. The thirty years can be looked upon as a period of spiritual unfoldment during the three divisions into which Aquarius (and consequently the New Age now upon us) will be divided. I refer to what is technically known as the three decans of each sign. In this sign the waters of the Piscean age will, symbolically speaking, be absorbed into the water-pot carried on the shoulder of Aquarius in the symbol which is distinctive of this sign, for Aquarius is the water-carrier, bringing the water of life to the people—life more abundantly.

In the Aquarian Age, the Risen Christ is Himself the Water-Carrier; He will not this time demonstrate the perfected life of a Son of God, which was His main mission before; He will appear as the supreme Head of the Spiritual Hierarchy, meeting the need of the thirsty nations of the world—thirsty for truth, for right human relations and for loving understanding. He will be recognised this time by all and in His Own Person will testify to the *fact* of the resurrection, and hence demonstrate the paralleling fact of the immortality of the soul, of the spiritual man. The emphasis during the past two thousand years has been *on death;* it has coloured all the teaching of the orthodox churches; only one day in the year has been dedicated to the thought of the resurrection. The emphasis in the Aquarian Age will be on life and freedom from the tomb of matter, and this is the note which will distinguish the new world religion from all that have preceded it.

The Festival of Easter and the Feast of Pentecost will be the two outstanding days of the religious year. Pentecost is, as you must well know, the symbol of right human relations in which all men and nations will understand each other and—though speaking in many and diverse languages —will know only one spiritual speech.

It is significant that two important episodes are related in the final part of the Gospel story—one preceding and one following immediately after the apparent death of Christ. They are:

1. The story of the upper chamber to which the man carrying the water pot and typifying Aquarius led the disciples, and in which the first communion service was held, participated in by all and foretelling that great relationship which will distinguish humanity in the coming age, after the tests of the Piscean Age. Such a communion service has never yet been held, but the New Age will see it take place.

2. The story of the upper chamber in which the disciples met and arrived at a true recognition of the Risen Christ and at a perfect and complete understanding of

each other in spite of the symbolic diversity of tongues. They had a touch of prevision, of prophetic insight, and foresaw a little of the wonder of the Aquarian Age. The vision in men's minds today is that of the Aquarian Age, even if they recognise it not. The future will see right relationships, true communion, a sharing of all things (wine, the blood, the life and bread, economic satisfaction) and goodwill; we have also a picture of the future of humanity when all nations are united in complete understanding and the diversity of languages—symbolic of differing traditions, cultures, civilisations and points of view —will provide no barrier to right human relations. At the centre of each of these pictures is to be found the Christ.

Thus the expressed aims and efforts of the United Nations will be eventually brought to fruition and a new church of God, gathered out of all religions and spiritual groups, will unitedly bring to an end the great heresy of separateness. Love, unity, and the Risen Christ will be present, and He will demonstrate to us the *perfect life*.

Training for new age

discipleship is provided

by the *Arcane School*.

The principles of the

Ageless Wisdom are

presented through esoteric

meditation, study and

service as a *way of life*.

*Write to the publishers
for information.*

INDEX

155